7/97

PHOBIAS

Everything You Wanted to Know, But Were Afraid to Ask

Judy Monroe

—Issues in Focus—

ENSLOW PUBLISHERS, INC.

44 Fadem Road	P.O. Box 38
Box 699	Aldershot
Springfield, N.J. 07081	Hants GU12 6BP
U.S.A.	U.K.

Library of Congress Cataloging-in-Publication Data

Monroe, Judy.
    Phobias: everything you wanted to know but were afraid to ask /
Judy Monroe.
        p. cm.— (Issues in focus)
    Includes bibliographical references and index.
    Summary: Describes phobias both common and uncommon through
examples and personal stories.
    ISBN 0-89490-723-9
    1. Phobias—Juvenile literature. [1. Phobias.] I. Title
II. Series: Issues in focus (Hillside, N.J.)
RC535.M625 1996
616.85'225—dc20   95-32931
                                              CIP
                                                AC

Printed in the United States of America

10 9 8 7 6 5 4 3 2 1

Photo Credits: Clay Bartl, pp. 11, 18, 23, 30, 34, 43, 47, 55, 60, 65, 69, 72, 76, 82; Judy Monroe, p. 7.

Illustration Credit: Clay Bartl, p. 51.

Cover Photo: The Stock Market, © 1987, Chris Collins.

Contents

1

Life Robbers

If you met Michelle* you would probably think she is like other high school seniors. She sparkles with fun and energy. She wants to get a part-time job and go to college. But look again and you will see a teen carefully taking one day at a time, as she tries to overcome her many phobias, her persistent extreme fears of certain objects or situations.

Michelle has never sat by herself through a full day of high school classes. She can trace her uncomfortable feelings about school back to kindergarten. As she got older, her feelings about school were so bad that by the eighth grade, her stomach would cramp up, her throat and chest would tighten, and she would often get dizzy and nauseated. These intense sick feelings, or panic attacks, eventually forced her to quit going to school.

*Not her real name.

5

Michelle developed other phobias, too. She avoided stores, shopping malls, and restaurants. She could not approach a drive-up window at a fast food restaurant. Waiting in line, whether in a car or on foot, was agony for her. She also feared staying home alone, visiting her friends, or sleeping over at a girlfriend's home. She never got her driver's license, she stopped going to the beach and football games, and never went to the prom. Eventually, she stopped getting into cars or taking trips, because she could no longer leave her home. Michelle's home became her jail.

Finally, Michelle got help for her phobias from a psychiatrist, a physician specializing in disorders of the mind. The psychiatrist prescribed Nardil™, an anti-depressant that helped Michelle deal with her panic attacks. A home-instruction teacher began working with Michelle in two areas: keeping up with school lessons and dealing with her various phobias.

A big day came when Michelle first rode in her teacher's car. Three weeks later, again with her teacher, Michelle was able to sit through a traffic light change. Next, the two went to a nearby store, and Michelle bought herself a blouse. After more counseling, Michelle sat through a few classes at school, went downtown to pick out her class ring, and to a mall—but always with her teacher.

Today, Michelle continues to get counseling and goes to a support group. She has taken enormous strides in handling her phobias. She now goes out with close friends, stays home alone, and visits with her friends. She loves music and goes to concerts with her sister. She plans to go back to high school next year, to finish her final year, and then to go to college. In 1994, Michelle

Some people are agoraphobic and cannot leave their homes. Their fears actually imprison them.

gave her mother a wonderful gift for Mother's Day: Michelle enjoyed a meal at a restaurant with her family![1]

Rational and Irrational Fears

Most of us can name at least one or two things we fear. Joe Eltgroth sometimes became a bit anxious when he had to cross a busy street on foot. It always took him a minute or two to look both ways several times, take some deep breaths, then hurry across the street. "It's really no big deal, though," Joe said. "I've always been able to cross a busy street and sometimes I don't even think about it."[2]

Joe's fear is rational, reasonable. A busy street can be dangerous to cross, and it makes sense to check carefully. However, when someone like Michelle becomes abnormally or irrationally afraid of objects, such as cars, or of situations, such as going to a shopping mall or going to school, then the fear is defined as a phobia.

The main element of a phobia is fear. A phobia is an irrational, abnormal, or exaggerated fear. Both fear and phobias cause psychological (mind) and physiological (body) changes.

Fear is a normal emotion. Fear and anxiety are feelings most of us experience at sometime during our lives. We may have an abnormal fear occasionally, but these fears usually do not keep us from carrying out our everyday activities. Remember your last big test? Even if you were well prepared, you probably still experienced some anxiety when your teacher handed out the test. Maybe you could not eat that morning, or you had a stomachache, or felt jumpy and nervous. Later, just before you saw your grade, your hands may have become sweaty, or your heart may have thumped a bit faster or seemed to thud louder. Those are normal reactions to a fearful situation. You had both uncomfortable emotional and physical reactions to your fear.

With phobias, the emotional and physical reactions are intensified. Phobics become abnormally terrified of an object or situation, even when they are in no real threat of danger. Their bodies react to fear in various ways such as sweating, shaking or trembling, or quick, shallow breathing. If they see that object, or if they are in that particular situation again, their bodies will react to their fear again. Many phobics freeze or, if possible, run away from or avoid the terrifying object or situation. This is often called the "fight or flight" reaction. If they continue to experience the phobia, or if it broadens in scope, phobics often start to think of themselves as strange or abnormal. People often will not talk about their terrifying fears, which tends to add to their anxiety and sense of oddness.

Here is an example of a simple fear that grew into a phobia with far-reaching consequences. Vicki was late for a business lunch and hurried into an elevator. She nearly fell when the elevator suddenly lurched to a stop between the sixteenth and seventeenth floors. She remembered:

> One second I was feeling only tiredness and hunger. The next second I was a raving maniac. I felt a terrible sick feeling in my stomach, my heart started to race a mile a minute, my legs felt as if they would give way. I became dizzy and faint. There was this terrible sensation of being enclosed in a solid steel box with no opening, suspended somewhere in space. I

panicked, pressed the alarm button, started screaming, clawed and banged at the doors. I thought I was going to go crazy or die.[3]

She was rescued, but unfortunately, this incident triggered her first attack of claustrophobia, the fear of enclosed spaces. Vicki could no longer ride in elevators. She quit her job because it was on the twenty-first floor. Her claustrophobia increased, and now she cannot go into airplanes, telephone booths, closed stairways, windowless rooms, or subways.

Focus on Phobias

Today, television and radio talk shows often feature people who talk about how they lived for years in their homes, afraid to step one foot outside their front doors. Some talk about how they finally overcame this fear, which is called agoraphobia. These stories catch our interest, but are these people unusual or uncommon?

Phobias are the most common mental health problem or disorder in the United States today, according to the American Psychiatric Association.[4] You probably would not recognize someone with a phobia, because most phobics maintain fairly normal lives. Most go to school or work, drive cars, go on dates, or marry. You may know of someone with a phobia, or you may have one yourself.

If you do, you are part of a large group of Americans. About 23 million people—one out of ten—say that they have a phobia.[5] So, in a room of one hundred people, at least ten have such intense, extreme fears that they could be called phobics. Of these people, about half must

Someone who is afraid of plants (botonophobic) may be allergic to them. This would be an example of a rational fear developing into a phobia.

organize their daily lives in some way so that they can handle their phobia, as Vicki did.[6] Many phobics cover and hide their fears and reactions so well that the casual observer does not know that they are phobic.

Not all phobias require treatment. Some phobias, though, can lead to serious problems. Fear of going to the dentist (dentophobia), for example, is a common phobia. Because of this phobia, millions of Americans suffer ongoing pain from toothaches, cavities, and gum diseases.[7] Left untreated, this can lead to major expense as even more serious dental problems develop.

The costs to people with severe phobias can run high. Some quit their jobs. Others drop out of school. Still others do not date, answer the telephone, or leave their houses. "They are among the heaviest users of the health-care system, and suffer from high rates of depression, and alcoholism, and are frequently suicidal," said Jerilyn Ross, president of the Anxiety Disorders Association of America (ADAA).[8]

For those who decide to get help, treatment is usually successful and can bring a new life to those who previously suffered. Many people with mild phobias treat themselves by using self-help books or other methods like phobia self-help groups. People with more serious phobias may require therapy.

First, though, phobics need to learn about their mental health problem. Although Jerilyn Ross has stated, "Millions of Americans remain in the dark about their condition," this is changing.[9] Many organizations provide education about phobias and offer treatment. The great majority of people can get control of their phobias and enjoy a full life.

2

More Than Fear

Phobias take many forms. Some people are afraid of snakes or spiders. Others are so afraid of public speaking that they cannot say one word during a class or a meeting. Some refuse to climb onto a city bus, get on an airplane, or take a subway. Still others avoid shopping malls, movie theaters, concerts, and any other places where crowds are likely to be. Because of their many overwhelming fears, some phobics have not stepped outside their home in years.

Not all people with phobias suffer such intense, crippling reactions to their fears. Some lead fairly normal lives. However, some people suffer because their phobias disrupt their lives. To escape their fears, they figure out any possible way to avoid the object, place, or situation that seems to cause their phobias. Here are three examples of people with phobias and how they dealt with them.

•Andy* started to feel anxious in high school classes when he was called on to give answers. His fears magnified in a college class where the professor randomly called on students to answer questions. To deal with his intense fear of public speaking, Andy cut classes, which led to problems in getting his college degree. Finally, he got help for his public speaking phobia from a therapist.[1]

•Amanda Warren admitted that she avoided crowds, including parties, because of her intense fear of groups of people. After therapy, Amanda delighted her friends when she showed up for a surprise birthday party. "I know for most people this may seem like nothing, but for me, it was a celebration," she said. It was her first party in nearly twenty-six years.[2]

•Barney* experienced a different phobia. He had always loved cats, dogs, and other farm animals and decided to become a veterinarian. While he was in veterinary school, he realized that he had a problem—a reptile phobia. He remembered thinking, "If it doesn't have hair, I don't want to handle it." He stayed away from reptiles, but eventually he was assigned to work at the veterinary school's exotic animal clinic, which cared for all kinds of reptiles. Instead of running from his phobia, Barney decided to attack his own fear. He learned all he could about reptiles, so that he could focus on facts, not on his terror. He also forced himself to spend time with snakes, lizards, and iguanas, so that he could observe and learn about them. He knew he had

*Not his real name.

beaten his phobia when someone brought in a sick iguana and he was able to handle and treat it.[3]

Andy, Amanda, and Barney all needed help to overcome their phobias. All three shared common traits when their phobias first appeared. First, they were extremely anxious in situations that were generally safe, such as speaking in a class or going to a party. Second, they avoided the source of their distress. Amanda always invented an excuse for not going to a party. Andy eliminated any chance of speaking in front of his classmates by not going to school.

Many phobics do not have to come in contact with what they fear to have phobic reactions. Instead, they often worry about possible fear-producing situations. For example, Andy could feel his heart race and his palms get sweaty when he even imagined himself speaking before his classmates.

When Does Fear Become a Phobia?

Fear is a normal response to a frightening situation. A pounding heart, rapid breathing, and trembling are all typical reactions to almost being hit by a car. This type of fear reaction is short-lived and is based on a real danger.

However, if people flee in great terror every time they see a spider or snake, or refuse ever to ride in a car, then the fear has grown into a phobia. "A phobia is an unrealistic fear that is all out of proportion to the actual threat," explained Anne Marie Albana, assistant director of the Center for Stress and Anxiety Disorders at the State University of New York at Albany. "The fear of spiders, for instance, would be present even when there were no spiders around. The most common fears people have are of animals or insects; natural elements like storms and water; and heights or closed-in spaces, like elevators."[4]

The American Psychiatric Association defines phobias this way: "The word *phobia* is a term that refers to a group of symptoms brought on by feared objects or situations. People can develop phobic reactions to animals [objects], social situations, and activities."[5] The object (a spider) or a situation (flying in an airplane) seldom does anything to the person. The person's extreme psychological and physical reactions to a spider or flying is called the phobic reaction.

Here is yet another definition by a therapist who specializes in treating phobics: "Fear becomes a phobia when it interferes with normal living and keeps you from doing things you want to do."[6]

Types of Phobias

Mental health professionals group phobias into three categories: specific phobias, social phobias, and agoraphobia. Although each causes strong, terrifying feelings for phobics, each type of phobia is different.

Specific Phobias

Sometimes called simple phobias, specific phobias are the most common type. Someone with a specific phobia has an unreasonable, persistent fear of a specific object or situation. Typical specific phobias include closed spaces, heights, bridges, flying, insects, storms, germs, and snakes. Most specific phobias focus on animals, natural phenomena (storms and thunder), and the human body.

16

Mild specific phobias generally do not cause many problems, but if they become severe, they can cause major life disturbances.

The most common specific phobia is fear of animals, especially of dogs, snakes, insects, and mice. (Animal phobias often begin during childhood but usually disappear during the teen or adult years.) People sometimes find that they can pinpoint when their animal phobia began. Keith Schooler remembers that, as a child, he helped collect eggs on his parents' farm in Zionsville, Indiana. One day, when he was about four years old, the biggest, crankiest rooster rushed toward him. Keith turned and ran away, terrified of the squawking bird with the flapping wings and slashing beak. After that, Keith began to fear all birds. By the time he went to college, he had outgrown his phobia of birds. A year ago, he even roomed with someone who owned a pet canary. "I'm still not crazy about birds, but I can be in the same room with them," Keith said.[7]

Natural phenomena phobias center on natural events such as earthquakes, floods, thunder, lightning, and storms. Dr. Stephen Garber reported that after a series of major California earthquakes, some children developed phobias. "Every aftershock sent people into panic. Many children had difficulty sleeping, feared separating from their parents for months, and remained anxious for some time."[8] To help deal with these extreme fears, the area schools established counseling programs.

Body phobias generally deal with a person's own body. Common body phobias include fear of pain (odynephobia), fear of blood (hematophobia or hemophobia), and fear of cancer (carcinophobia). Unlike

17

Phobias often develop from traumatic situations. Keith's horrifying experience with birds led to the development of his ornithophobia —the fear of birds.

animal and natural phobias, reactions to body phobias sometimes include a rapid drop in blood pressure, sometimes followed by fainting.

Social Phobias

Instead of fearing specific things, people with social phobias fear situations that involve people. For some of us, falling down could be a little embarrassing. To a social phobic, though, actually falling or thinking about falling causes intense terror.

Social phobics have an intense fear of situations in which their activities could be watched and judged by others. They hate to look or act stupid, and because they get so anxious about their performance, they sometimes perform poorly in public. Their real or imagined bad performance then intensifies their worries. Some social phobics feel such stress about possible embarrassing situations that they spend a lot of time and energy avoiding any threatening public activities. Others will go ahead with the threatening activities, but will suffer terrible anxiety before, during, and after the event.

Shyness and social phobias are not the same. Shy people often feel self-conscious. They may feel uncomfortable meeting or talking with strangers, but can force themselves to do so if necessary. Social phobics are more than shy. They avoid any situation with people they feel are scary or threatening and also become very anxious before and during any public event.

The most common social phobia, according to the American Psychiatric Association, is speaking in public. The list of other potentially threatening activities for social phobics seems endless: dating, eating or drinking in a restaurant, using a public restroom, casual conversations (especially with strangers), blushing, going to a party or nightclub, dancing, buttoning a coat, signing a personal check or credit card slip, coughing during a concert or play, choking on popcorn during a movie, falling while ice skating, playing a game of basketball—just about any activity near or involving people.

Some social phobics worry that their hands or head will shake as they eat, write, or perform other daily activities. This leads them to avoid banks, restaurants, and other public places. They often do not maintain much eye contact when talking with others and will cross the street to avoid talking with an approaching friend or acquaintance. Parties rate high on their list of things to avoid, and they prefer to do things alone, away from the eyes of others.

Social phobics generally avoid playing sports, especially competitive games. Sometimes athletes form a phobia as a reaction to the constant pressure to perform well. For example, a professional football player, formerly an excellent athlete, could no longer kick well during a live game, when tens of thousands of cheering fans watched. His kicks became short, wobbly, and off the mark. During practice, with no fans around, his kicks were great—long and accurate. Therapy helped him overcome his social phobia and return to his position.[9]

John* is another person with a social phobia. His phobia affects every part of his life. As a child, John was rather shy and quiet, but he laughed and played games with his friends. By his early teens, John began withdrawing from his friends. He went to fewer and fewer parties and concerts and preferred to

*Not his real name.

study or to listen to music alone in his room. Always an excellent student, John was accepted into a top-ranked college. He packed his suitcases, said good-bye to his parents, and left home to live in a dorm. He did not make a single friend and stopped going out of his room except for quickly-eaten meals. Finally, unable to cope with any part of college life, John dropped out before the end of the first semester and returned to live at his parents' home. He feels the safest when he is alone in his room, listening to music.

John described what it was like for him in college:

> Every time I walked into a classroom I would start sweating profusely, my mouth felt like it was full of cotton, and I didn't think I would be able to talk—even if my life depended on it. Then I would start to feel this intense heat rise up through my arms and legs and face and I would turn bright red—as if my entire body was blushing.[10]

John's type of social phobia "is so severe that it interferes with daily functioning, at work, at school, and in almost all interpersonal relationships (except the immediate family). It is a shyness that is so emotionally painful that many who suffer from the disorder shun any kind of social contact," explained the therapist who works with John.[11]

Agoraphobia

Agoraphobics often experience one of three terrifying fears: fear of being alone, fear of leaving home, or fear of being caught someplace where it is hard or awkward to leave. Agoraphobics are afraid of being in public places if they think escape is impossible or difficult.

Someone with agoraphobia may seem to have the same symptoms as someone with a social phobia. Both, for example, may not go to parties, but their reasons for not going differ. Social phobics fear people looking at them and judging their clothes or their hair, or they cannot talk to strangers.

Agoraphobics avoid parties for a different reason. They have an intense fear of a panic attack occurring at the party. They also fear that they will lose control over their bodies. Panic attacks are unexpected and unexplained periods when someone reacts to an extreme fear; however nothing specific has caused that fear. Panic attacks seem to have no cause and hit suddenly, with no warning. Although they usually last for only a few minutes, they can cause intense, frightening feelings and body changes. Not all people will have all these symptoms, but at least four of the following symptoms will usually appear during a panic attack: a racing heart, shortness of breath, chest pains, sweating, heart pounding, fainting, dizziness, hot or cold flashes, trembling or shaking, nausea, tingling, and weakness. For many, a terrible fear takes over during the panic attack—that they will go crazy, completely lose control, or die. About one third of those who suffer from panic attacks will eventually develop agoraphobia.

Agoraphobics display a wide range of intense fears. Some stop using public transportation or going to a shopping mall or supermarket, because they fear being trapped in a public place. Others shy away from wide-open spaces and will not drive down wide streets or walk in a large, open field. Long hallways in buildings scare some agoraphobics. Some cannot leave their own homes

Some agoraphobics can no longer use city buses or other public transportation because they fear being trapped inside the vehicle.

to go anyplace unless they are with a trusted friend or relative. Some can only travel on a fixed route, from home to work or school, then back home. Other agoraphobics have not stepped outside their homes in months or years. Until she went to a therapist for treatment, one woman with severe agoraphobia had not gone beyond the boundaries of her house and yard in forty years.

Agoraphobics tend to avoid situations or places that they think may bring on a panic attack. They also fear that they will not be able to quickly get to a place where they feel safe or to a person with whom they feel comfortable. For some agoraphobics, only a handful of places are terrifying, but for others, nearly every place holds a threat of danger.

What Kind of Person Has Phobias?

Phobias strike more women than men. A large study by the National Institutes of Mental Health (NIMH) and the Anxiety Disorders Association of America found that up to 12 percent of Americans have phobias. The researchers also found that phobias were the most common mental health problem among women of all ages and the second most common mental health problem among men older than twenty-five.[12]

Specific phobias, especially animal phobias, are common in children. However, anyone can develop a specific phobia at any age. Just over 11 percent of Americans have a specific phobia, but females are twice as likely as men to develop them.[13]

More than 13 percent of Americans have social phobias.[14] Social phobias generally take hold more slowly than do simple phobias or agoraphobia. Social phobias often start when people are between the ages of fifteen and twenty, and they affect slightly more females than males. People may suffer from only one social phobia, or they may have several at one time.

Social phobics generally have limited school, work, and social lives, because they interact poorly with other people. If they are untreated, social phobics can develop agoraphobia, alcoholism, or depression. Some social phobics may become suicidal; they sometimes try to take their own lives.

A little more than 5 percent of Americans have agoraphobia, the most disabling phobia.[15] It usually starts when the phobic person is between the ages of eighteen and thirty-five, and it affects nearly three times more women than men. It can start suddenly or slowly. There is no single type of person who develops agoraphobia.

Superstitions, Hypochondria, and Phobias

Phobias are not related to superstitions or hypochondria. A superstition is an irrational belief that an object, action, or circumstance will influence the outcome of an unrelated event. Superstitions are widely known and shared by many people. People generally do not have panic attacks because of their superstitions. Usually, people suffer no lasting or harmful effects from their superstitions. If someone avoids black cats on Halloween, for example, this superstition lasts a short time—about twenty-four hours. A phobia lasts much longer than a day.

Hypochondriacs have persistent thoughts that they are ill or likely to become ill. They suffer real pain although a physical illness is neither present nor likely. They usually see a lot of doctors. Hypochondria often begins when a person is a teenager, but it tends to get worse in their thirties and forties. Hypochondriacs' symptoms remain vague and chronic and often move to different body parts.

Someone with an illness phobia reacts differently than a hypochondriac. An illness phobic has an unreasonable fear of a specific illness, such as cancer or AIDS. This person's extreme fear is sometimes triggered when a close friend or relative develops the illness.

What Phobias Feel Like

Carol Schatz had a driving phobia that started when she was in her late twenties. She described it this way:

> You're at the wheel and your stomach is slightly queasy. A soft but steady ringing starts in your ears. You try to get a grip—in this case, on the wheel. You tell yourself it's fine, you know how to drive, you've never crashed. . . . When you force yourself to start driving, your head feels like it's filling with helium and is desperately trying to detach itself from your body. Your heart is making far too much noise.[16]

Fred, a social phobic, was required to take Spanish in the seventh grade. This was a terrible experience for him, because he had to speak the language in front of his classmates and teacher. He remembered:

> I performed very poorly and was always embarrassed. I could barely get the words out and knew all the

26

other students noticed my problem. My heart would beat fast, my hands would sweat and my mind would become dizzy. Every morning I woke up with a stomachache and a general frightened anxious feeling.[17]

Many people with phobias feel a little anxious most of the time. They worry a lot, even when they are not aware of doing so. Not all phobics experience the same symptoms when they become afraid, and their symptoms can vary during each phobic reaction.

When their fear is triggered, phobics can feel dizzy or anxious, and they can shake, faint, tremble, or sweat. Their stomachs may churn, and they may feel nauseated, hot, or numb. Some have trouble standing because of wobbly knees. They can have breathing difficulties or feel confused or out of control. Most will feel strong and irrational panic, dread, horror, or terror and will want to—or actually do—run from the fearful object or situation. These overwhelming symptoms may cause some phobics to fear that they are dying, are having a heart attack, or are going crazy.

After their intense fear reaction, many phobics feel tired and shaky. If this is a first attack, they may feel alarmed. For longtime phobics, an attack often brings anger or embarrassment, because they could not prevent the attack.

Related Problems

The physical and emotional pain caused by severe phobias brings much suffering to the phobic. Other problems tend to multiply as a result of the phobia.

Some people with phobias resort to drinking or taking drugs to help them cope. Researchers report that about 20 percent of social phobics and agoraphobics develop alcoholism, and about half of those suffer from depression.[18]

Phobias may cause some people to lose self-esteem. Many phobics silently yell and scold themselves for not being strong enough to overcome their fears. Because they can no longer work, some phobics slide into poverty. Family members, friends, and coworkers may not understand or believe how bad the phobic feels. Relationships and friendships sometimes dissolve and families can fall apart.

One young woman still feels sad because she could not leave her home to take her baby son to a nearby park or for rides in his stroller. "The thought of opening the front door was enough to give me the shakes," she said. "I let agoraphobia steal the joy from my life for nine years."[19]

Famous Phobics

Some famous people have suffered from phobias, including:

Carly Simon, singer and songwriter, who could not perform live for eight years because of topophobia, or severe stage fright.[20]

Willard Scott, who was a social phobic before he became a well-known television weather forecaster. He has explained being shy and having a social phobia this way: "I compare it to cutting your fingers as opposed to having a train run over you. The difference is that dramatic."[21]

Harry Houdini, world-famous escape artist, who was claustrophobic. He could cope well when locked into tight spaces during his escape acts. However, when he accidentally was trapped in tight spaces, he had phobic reactions.[22]

Phil Donahue, popular television talk show host, who has aerophobia, the fear of flying. On one show, he told his viewers that the more he flies, the more anxious he becomes.[23]

Aretha Franklin, singer, who is also aerophobic.[24]

Frederick the Great, eighteenth-century king of Prussia, who could not wash himself because he was terrified of water (aquaphobia; hydrophobia). His servants cleaned him with dry towels.[25]

Napoleon Bonaparte, emperor of France and conqueror of many other lands, who was terrified of cats (ailurophobia).[26]

Edgar Allan Poe, author, who feared closed spaces. He drew on his own claustrophobic reactions when he wrote some of his great short stories, such as the "The Black Cat" and "The Premature Burial."[27]

Sigmund Freud, who became world famous for his creation of psychoanalysis, a form of therapy. He often wrote about his own agoraphobia. He also feared death, traveling by train, and crossing wide streets.[28]

Howard Hughes, who probably was the most famous and wealthy phobic of this century. First, he developed a fear of germs (microphobia) and always wore gloves before touching anyone. He went through four boxes of tissue paper every day, because he wiped off everything

Anyone can develop a phobia. Even Napolean Bonaparte had one: ailurophobia, the fear of cats.

he touched or received. As he grew older, he became agoraphobic. Finally, he become panphobic—afraid of everything and everyone. For example, Howard Hughes "saw a 189-foot-high one-million-dollar sign in front of the hotel across the street. He was immediately convinced it was going to fall on his penthouse. When the owners refused to take down the sign, Hughes bought the hotel."[29]

3

A Long History

Phobias have been described throughout ancient and modern history. People have written about them in many parts of the world. At first, phobias were often called "fear sickness." The word *phobia* was not used in medical literature until the late eighteenth century.

Phobia comes from the Greek word *phobos* which means fear, terror, panic, and flight. In Greek mythology, Phobos was a Greek god who caused fear and panic in his enemies during war. Warriors used the power of this fear by carrying into battle shields etched with Phobos's picture. He was shown with a beard and horns. Although phobias and phobic reactions have been recorded for thousands of years, a scientific understanding first began in the twentieth century.

Early History

Hippocrates (hih PAHK ru teez) lived from about 460 to about 377 B.C., and is known as the father of medicine. He recorded detailed descriptions of people with phobias. Over two thousand three-hundred years ago, he wrote of a man named Damocles (DAM uh kleez) who could not go near an overhang, or over a bridge, or even near a shallow body of water. Another friend, Nicaros (NI ka rus), happily listened to flute music during the day. However, at night, Nicaros could not listen to anyone playing a flute without feeling extreme fear. Hippocrates described how Nicaros reacted. "As soon as he heard the first note of the flute at a banquet, he would be beset by terror, and said he could scarcely contain himself."[1]

In 1621, in his book *Anatomy of Melancholy*, English clergyman Robert Burton wrote in great detail of people with various intense fears. Some could not leave their homes for fear that they would faint, become sick, or die. Another could not cross a bridge, or go near water or steep hills. He also described a person who was afraid of being locked in rooms and who could not go into crowds or public places.

During Robert Burton's lifetime (1577–1640), much fearful and unusual behavior was thought to be caused by witchcraft, demons, or evil spirits.[2] A little later, John Bunyan (1628-1688), English author of *The Pilgrim's Progress*, described his own increasing fear of ringing bells and church steeples. At first, he worried that the bell would fall straight on him. Then he feared that the bell would bounce off the wall and kill him. His fear continued to grow until he actually thought the

33

Throughout the centuries, some people have feared bridges. This phobia may actually represent a fear of being trapped or a fear of heights. Gephyrophobia was noted as long ago as the time of Hippocrates.

steeple would come crashing down, fall on his head, and kill him.[3]

A. Le Camus (lae ka MOO), a French surgeon who lived from 1722 to 1772, wrote the first comprehensive medical study on phobias in 1769. He named his book *Des Aversions.* Samuel Johnson (1709–1784), an English author, noted his own fear of crowded places. He asked to be excused from jury duty because he would nearly faint in crowded places. Benjamin Rush (1745–1813), a noted American doctor, wrote an article in 1789 that gave his definition of phobias: "I shall define phobia to be a fear of an imaginary evil, or an undue fear of a real one."[4] His definition is still used today. He also named eighteen specific phobias, including fear of dirt and fear of rats.

Greater Understanding

During the 1800s, people began to study how the mind works. Phobias were increasingly described in psychiatric studies and writings. Psychiatry is the branch of medicine that deals with the diagnosis, treatment, and prevention of mental and emotional disorders. The first definition of agoraphobia was published in 1872 by Otto Westphal (1833–1890) in his book *Die Agoraphobie.* He described three people with agoraphobia. Each person dreaded and avoided walking through certain streets or areas in town, especially when the streets were deserted and all the stores were closed. All felt more comfortable walking in these areas if trusted people came with them. One agoraphobic drank alcohol to give him courage to deal with his fears.

Westphal decided to use the word *agoraphobia* to describe this fear. His patients had a terrible phobia of streets or public places. *Agora* is the Greek word for "market." He also noted that the thought of going to these places was as terrifying to these people as actually going. He accurately described typical reactions of agoraphobics. His paper caught the attention of researchers and doctors in France, England, and Germany.

For several decades, people wrote about and named many phobias. Many of those names are still used today. In Austria, Sigmund Freud (1856–1939) contributed great work on understanding phobias in the late 1800s. He was one of the first people to describe the feelings of anxiety that occur with phobic reactions. Others added their knowledge of the causes and treatment of phobias.

During the late 1970s, research on the brain and brain chemistry helped scientists better understand human behavior and emotions. Along with research on mental health, this research led to increased knowledge about phobias. Researchers and therapists developed better definitions of phobias for the *Diagnostic and Statistical Manual of Mental Disorders (DSM)*, a book that helps doctors, psychiatrists, psychologists, and others who need to know the definition and diagnosis of phobias and other mental disorders. The *DSM* was first published in 1952 and listed all the types of mental disorders known at that time. It was revised in 1968, 1980, and 1987. Social phobia was listed in the 1980 manual. Before then, scientists called it shyness. The *DSM* manual was last revised in early 1994. It includes definitions for three types of phobias: specific phobia, social phobia, and panic disorder with agoraphobia.[5]

In the early 1980s, researchers gathered information on the number of Americans suffering from phobias. At that time, the National Institutes of Mental Health (NIMH) conducted the first survey of mental health in the United States, the Epidemiological Catchment Area (ECA) survey. Researchers interviewed nearly twenty thousand people in five cities: Baltimore, Maryland; New Haven, Connecticut; St. Louis, Missouri; Durham, North Carolina; and Los Angeles, California. This survey uncovered a startling fact: Anxiety disorders, including all phobias, are the most common mental health problem in the United States.

The results of a more current nationwide study, the National Comorbidity Survey (NCS), agreed with the results of the ECA survey. Since these studies were published, people have heard and seen a lot of information about phobias in newspaper and magazine articles, on television and radio, and in books and pamphlets. The NIMH spends millions of dollars each year on the causes and treatments of phobias and other anxiety disorders. This information has reached many people with phobias, and it has helped them understand their phobias and the various treatments available.

4

An A to Z List of Phobias

Although more than two hundred phobias have been named, researchers have found that about one hundred phobias account for most people's fears. Phobias often get their names from Latin. For example, the Latin word for "bee" is *api*. So the fear of bees is *api* + *phobia* or *apiphobia.*

People can develop phobias about nearly anything. Since ancient times, people all over the world have had phobias about things, places, and situations. In our rapidly changing modern world, people develop phobias about things that did not even exist hundreds of years ago. Cyberphobia, for example, has grown within the last few years, as computers have become part of our everyday lives. Fear of flying is a common phobia, but airplanes were still a dream until the Wright brothers' flying machines launched a whole new industry.

All people with phobias share one important thing in common—intense fear. Many people have overcome their phobias, either on their own or through some type of help and support.

IF THE FEAR IS OF . . .	THEN THAT PHOBIA IS CALLED . . .
air, wind, or strong drafts	anemophobia
animals	zoophobia
beards	pogonophobia
bees	apiphobia
being by oneself	eremophobia, eremiophobia, ermitophobia
being buried alive	taphophobia, taphephobia
bicycles	cyclophobia
birds; feathers	ornithophobia
blood	hermatophobia, hemophobia
books	bibliophobia
bridges	gephyrophobia
burglars; stealing	kleptophobia, cleptophobia (harpaxophobia is the fear of becoming a victim of robbers)
cancer	carcinophobia, cancerphobia
cats	ailurophobia
choking	pnigophobia, pnigerophobia
cities	cosmophobia
clocks, passage of time	chronophobia
closed places	claustrophobia
clouds	nephophobia

IF THE FEAR IS OF . . .	THEN THAT PHOBIA IS CALLED . . .
cold	cryophobia
colors	chromatophobia
computers	cyberphobia
crossing streets	agyiophobia, dromophobia
crowds	ochlophobia, demophobia, enochlophobia
dancing	chorophobia
dawn	eosophobia
daylight	phengophobia
dentists	dentophobia
disorder	ataxiophobia
doctors	iatrophobia
dogs	cynophobia
dolls, children	pedophobia
dreams	oneirophobia
electricity	electrophobia
empty spaces	kenophobia
everything	panphobia
eyes	ommatophobia
failure	kakorrhaphiophobia
fear	phobophobia
fire	pyrophobia
fish	icthyophobia
floods	antlophobia
flying	aerophobia
fog	homichlophobia
food	sitophobia
funerals	threnophobia
fur	doraphobia

IF THE FEAR IS OF . . .	THEN THAT PHOBIA IS CALLED . . .
germs	microphobia
getting fat	lipophobia
hair	trichopathophobia, trichophobia
hats	mitrophobia
heart disease	cardiophobia
heights	acrophobia, hypsophobia
horses	hippophobia, equinophobia
illness	nosemaphobia, nosophobia
injury	traumatophobia
insanity	dementophobia
insects	entomophobia
light	photophobia
lightning	astraphobia, astrapophobia, keraunophobia
machinery	mechanophobia
marriage	gamophobia
medicine	pharmacophobia
mice and rats	musophobia
mirrors	spectrophobia
money	chrematophobia
moon	selenophobia
moving or making changes	tropophobia, neophobia
mushrooms	mycophobia
music	musicophobia, melophobia
needles and pins	belonephobia
night	nyctophobia
nosebleeds	epistaxiophobia
number thirteen	triskaidekaphobia

IF THE FEAR IS OF . . .	THEN THAT PHOBIA IS CALLED . . .
numbers	numerophobia
old age	gerascophobia
open spaces, unfamiliar places	agoraphobia
outer space	astrophobia, stratophobia
pain	odynesphobia, odynophobia
paper	papyrophobia
plants	botonophobia
poverty	peniaphobia
public speaking	is a form of social phobia; also called performance anxiety, topophobia (stage fright)
rain	ombrophobia
reptiles	batrachophobia
robbers	harpaxophobia
school	scolinophobia
shadows	sciophobia
sharks	selachophobia
slime	blennophobia
smothering	pnigophobia
snakes	ophidiophobia
snow	chionophobia
spiders	arachnophobia
stars	siderophobia
strangers	xenophobia
sun	heliophobia
technology	technophobia
teeth	odonophobia
thinking	phronemophobia

Fear of snow is known as chionophobia. Some phobics associate it with suffering or death.

IF THE FEAR IS OF . . .	THEN THAT PHOBIA IS CALLED . . .
thunder	brontophobia
trees	dendrophobia
vegetables	lachanophobia
vehicles	amaxophobia, ochophobia
walking	basiphobia
wasps	spheksophobia
water	aquaphobia, hydrophobia
wolves	lycophobia
women	gynephobia
worms	vermiphobia, scoleciphobia
writing	graphophobia

Some Common Phobias

Acrophobia, hypsophobia— A fear of heights is one of the most common phobias in the United States. More than 8 million people suffer from this fear, but few seek treatment. People with acrophobia fear being on the top floors of buildings or at the top of a hill or mountain. Many get nervous if they are near or on bridges, rooftops, and overlooks. People often develop this phobia because they are afraid of falling from a tall place and hurting themselves. Sometimes they may actually want to jump off a tall place, to get away from it.

Mildred has never gone inside a skyscraper, but then Mildred fears just standing on a chair. When she was a student librarian, she broke into a sweat every time she had to climb a ladder to reach a high shelf. She has arranged her lifestyle around her severe phobia, which has followed her since she was a child. Mildred's home has one floor and no basement. She chose to be a children's librarian because that collection of books is usually on the first floor or in the basement of a library. She will not go to a party if she has to climb stairs or use an elevator. She has not seen a live sports event in years because she cannot sit in the bleachers. Crossing bridges (gephyrophobia) is out of the question for Mildred. That is because "in any of these situations, Mildred imagines she would be drawn over the edge and would not be able to resist the impulse to plunge or fall from the height."[1]

Aerophobia—One of the most common phobias in the world is fear of flying. This can add up to a lot of problems, especially for people who need to travel by air because of their jobs. Pathway Systems, a program that helps people overcome their fear of flying, estimates that business travelers with aerophobia avoid some 6 million flights a year.

Many aerophobics will not even go near an airplane. They list many reasons to be concerned: They could get sick on a rough flight, the airplane could crash, no one would control the airplane if the pilot got ill, or they could die. They worry that they will lose control in the airplane and embarrass themselves or go crazy. Others fear death or being separated from loved ones. Some fear being trapped and being unable to leave the airplane, being rejected by others on the flight, and giving up control to the air crew. These reasons reflect specific fears such as fear of being alone, fear of being rejected by others, and fear of being trapped and hurt.

Treatment for aerophobia works well, especially when people get accurate information about airplanes and flying. Some local airports sponsor courses for people who are afraid to fly. One popular national treatment program is USAir's™ Fearful Flyer Program. Every year, the airline offers this program in cities across the United States. Classes, each led by a clinical social worker and a pilot, have helped thousands of people through aviation education, relaxation techniques, and a short flight.

Hillary decided to try a similar treatment program when her fear of flying developed into a phobia. As a kid, Hillary loved to go on airplanes. "I loved the smell of jet fuel, the peanuts, the playing cards, the free cans of Coke™," she remembers. Somehow, she started to fear flying. One day, when she was about twenty, she was on a rocky flight and became panic-stricken, afraid she would die during the flight. After that, she developed all kinds of rituals to help her through a flight, such as carrying good-luck charms or sitting only in certain spots on the airplane. Her flying companions got tired of sympathizing with her fears. Finally, four years later, she realized that she had a phobia and enrolled in a three-day workshop called Freedom from Fear.

The goal for her group of twelve people was to fly from New York to Boston and back by the third day of the workshop. First the group learned technical information about flying; then they practiced ways to cope with their fears, such as deep breathing and relaxing. Next, all twelve got on the plane and explored the controls, opened the doors and windows and walked around, to help make them more comfortable on the airplane. Finally, everyone took the trip and did fine. After taking other flights since then, Hillary says she is not crazy about flying, but still likes the peanuts. [2]

Agoraphobia—This fear has been recognized since ancient times as fear of "the market place." Agoraphobics fear leaving familiar homes or places. They dislike going

46

Fear of flying is one of the common phobias in the United States and throughout much of the world.

into streets, unknown buildings, city buses or cars, or crowded places, because they fear panic attacks. To increase their comfort level, some agoraphobics prefer to go to unknown places with people they trust and know well, in case they panic. Current studies have found that nearly 75 percent of agoraphobics are women. According to Dr. Ronald Doctor, "Agoraphobia is the most common phobic disorder for which people seek treatment. It is also the most disabling."[3]

Ailurophobia—For most people, soft, furry cats make great pets. Ailurophobics would disagree, however. They say that cats can scratch or hurt them, or that they dislike a cat's large eyes staring at them. People with cat phobias generally avoid cats, but if they see a picture or photo of a cat, or see or touch a live cat, they panic. They may have a hard time breathing, and their hearts may race. These phobic reactions may appear to be the same as an allergic reaction to a cat, but they are not. An allergy is when the body physically reacts badly to a specific substance. Allergic reactions include trouble breathing, rashed, sneezing, itchy and watery eyes, and stomach problems.

Amaxophobia, ochophobia—Sometimes people are afraid of driving or riding in vehicles, usually because of claustrophobia. Jerry's fear of taxis threatened his income, because he was a taxi driver. He started out driving in New York City, but he became increasingly terrified when he had to drive through the city's tunnels. He admitted to being claustrophobic, and he knew the reason for this. As a child, he was locked in a dark closet when he misbehaved. His fear spread to enclosed phone booths and elevators, and then to tunnels.

Jerry moved to another city, hoping to leave his fears behind. Instead, he now could not go to the movies or to church unless he sat in the aisle seat, and he did not go to other public places unless he felt he could easily escape. He continued to avoid elevators, but now he feared stairs. He then realized that he could no longer drive his taxi in heavy traffic. When his fear grew so that he could not sit behind the wheel of his cab, he sought treatment, because "that job was the only thing I knew how to do."[4]

Apiphobia—The fear of bees often starts with a general fear of flying insects. Children start fearing flying insects from watching others react or by seeing scary movies about bees or flying insects. People who are afraid of bees report that the tiny yellow-and-black insects are attacking them. If people have an extreme fear of bees, they drive with the car windows always tightly rolled up, or they stay indoors during the day. As with ailurophobia, people who are allergic to bee stings differ from apiphobics. In fact, bee stings can be fatal to some people who are allergic.

Aquaphobia, hydrophobia—This phobia was described as early as the first century A.D. People with this phobia are afraid of water. Some people fear swimming, bathing, or seeing or imagining running water or bodies of water such as lakes, streams, or rivers. Sometimes people cannot go into water over their heads, although they know how to swim. Others avoid being on the water's surface and stay away from boats, canoes, or ships. Carol Murray refuses to take showers and only bathes in a bathtub. She explained, "I feel panicky in a shower. I don't like the water hitting my face and running down my body. My heart starts to race and my breathing gets short and choppy. I'll go into a pool, but only if the water is lower than my waist." [5]

Aquaphobics' fear often began when they were babies or small children. They may have nearly drowned in a pool or in a larger body of water. Parents or grandparents may have taught the child the fear by demonstrating it themselves, or by forcing the child into deep water before he or she could swim.

Arachnophobia—At one time, spiders played a role in medicine. To cure fevers, doctors in the mid-eighteenth century recommended eating spiders spread on top of bread and butter. [6] Today, the fear of spiders affects more females than males. People with strong arachnophobia try to avoid spiders by fumigating their homes regularly (treating with fumes to kill pests). They carefully wash all fruits and vegetables, and they check all bags and boxes for any hidden spiders. For some people, this fear may be based on a widely held myth. Many people believe that spiders are poisonous, but few deadly spiders actually exist in the United States. [7]

Astraphobia, keraunophobia—People who fear lightning often will not go outside during storms, or if lightning is predicted. They check the weather reports often. If lightning occurs, they may hide in small, tight places such as closets, or they may hide under beds. Some people develop this fear from observing the reactions of parents or grandparents who are afraid of lightning. Other people may have a bad experience with lightning during a storm.

Batrachophobia—If you fear snakes and frogs, you have bactrachophobia, a fear of reptiles. Some people react to pictures, descriptions, or the sight of these animals;

Many of the people who suffer from arachnophobia hold the misguided belief that most spiders are poisonous.

they fear their webbed feet, long hind legs, and skin. Others simply fear actually touching these creatures.

Botonophobia—Have you ever heard that people who are ill should not have flowers left in their rooms at night? Some phobics believe this myth. This idea may have developed in ancient times, from fairy tales told to children about plants and flowers that were hiding places for evil spirits. During the night, the evil spirits would sneak out and hurt the sick person. Some botonophobics say that plants use up oxygen needed by people. Some people with pollen and other plant allergies develop botonophobia because they fear the rashes, sneezing, and other symptoms caused by their plant allergies.

Brontophobia—Although some people find thunderstorms exciting, brontophobics avoid thunder whenever possible. They may call the weather forecast numbers or radio stations to determine if and when thunder is approaching. If it is predicted, they often stay home. During episodes of thunder, some brontophobics hide in small spaces, as astraphobics do.

Claustrophobia—Many people dislike feeling trapped. However, people with claustrophobia actually panic when they are in a closed place. Many report that they cannot breathe; they feel as though they are suffocating. Claustrophobics react to all types of places: closets, subways, tunnels, telephone booths, caves, elevators, small rooms, crowds, cars, buses, airplanes, and many types of buildings. Some claustrophobics can manage a few specific enclosed spaces—cars or buses, but not trains, for example. Crowds, or even the thought of crowds, brings terror to people with claustrophobia. They avoid crowds and severely limit their activities. Sometimes claustrophobics can handle being in an enclosed place, as long as a door is left open. Others may panic if they are in a room with a shut window or if the window shade, blind, or curtain covers the window.

Sometimes claustrophobia results from a frightening dream of being trapped in a closed space. When the person awakens, the dream may be forgotten, but the feelings of fear remain. For others, a real-life experience may trigger claustrophobia. Bonnie remembers that as a young girl, she could not find her mother at home. She went to a neighbor's house to look for her mother. Not hearing anyone, she began walking through the neighbor's house. When she climbed into the attic, the door, perhaps caught by the wind, slammed shut. She could not open it, and she sat in the hot, dusty room all day. Frightened and hungry, she could not get out or signal for help. Bonnie was finally rescued when the neighbors came looking for her in a neighborhood search. Decades later, Bonnie still fears being in a room with a closed door and no windows.[8]

Cryophobia—Imagine how it would be if you lived in northern Minnesota, where the temperature often dips below zero during the winter, and you were cryophobic. Cryophobics fear cold or cold objects. They may fear cold weather, being outdoors in the winter, or not being able to stay warm enough during the winter. Sometimes these people will overdress to stay warm. Some people who fear cold avoid adding ice to drinks or drinking cold beverages at all.

Cyberphobia—Most of us would have a hard time avoiding computers today. However, some people fear, distrust, or even hate computers. If they are forced to work with computers, they may sweat a lot, become dizzy or nauseated, and have trouble breathing. Their blood pressure skyrockets. Many cyberphobics struggle to hide their fears, since they must work with computers during school or in their jobs.

Cynophobia—Some people do not think that dogs are people's best friends. Cynophobics fear dogs, perhaps because they remind them of wolves or jackals. Others dislike a dog's smell, fur, barking, and tendency to be noisy and destructive. Many cynophobics find that their fear comes from being bitten or snapped at by a dog when they were children.

Dentophobia—Some people fear dentists so much that they would rather suffer severe tooth pain than seek dental help. Therapists find that such a strong fear of dentists can often be traced to a bad dental experience in childhood. Someone with mild dental fear will have a dry mouth, sweaty palms, and a faster than normal heart rate. Those with high dental fear do not breathe well; this alone can bring on light-headedness and increased anxiety. Some people will actually jump out of the dental chair and run out of the room, especially at the sight or sound of the dentist's drill.

Such anxiety is no joke. The American Dental Association estimates that 35 million Americans have some form of dentophobia but will still visit their dentist. Those people with strong dentophobia will not seek dental care, sometimes for decades at a time.[9]

Entomophobia—An enormous variety of insects inhabit the earth. Unfortunately, some people fear these tiny creatures so much that they can never open their

Although we are now in the Information Age, some people are terrified of computers and avoid using them whenever possible.

windows. They even may seal the windows shut. They may vacuum and sweep several times a day, hoping to catch any stray insects that wandered into their house or apartment. Some entomophobics seldom leave their clean and safe homes for fear of seeing or being touched by an insect. They get their homes fumigated regularly. People sometimes focus on a particular type of insect, such as butterflies or dragonflies, because they are afraid of flying insects. Entomophobics often say that they dislike insects so much because they bite, cause itching, or carry disease.

Eremophobia—People who never *want* to be alone sometimes *fear* being alone. For some, this fear is worse if they are sick or in pain. Sometimes this fear is wrapped in other fears, such as the fear of becoming old (gerascophobia). Bejamin Rush (1745–1837), a noted American doctor, called eremophobia "solo phobia."

Gephyrophobia—People who are afraid to cross bridges actually may fear being trapped. They also may be afraid of being in narrow spaces, or they may fear heights. For gephyrophobics, trying to cross a bridge causes them to gasp for breath, break into a sweat, and get weak in the legs so that they cannot walk well. Many cannot cross a bridge, whether on foot or in a bus or car.

Hematophobia, hemophobia—Some people feel a bit queasy at the sight of blood. Some look away when they are about to get an injection by a doctor or nurse. For hematophobics, the sight or thought of blood causes a deep fear. People with this phobia or injury phobias (traumatophobia) usually go through all the feelings and symptoms of those with other phobias, but with one difference: When they are afraid, their heart rate increases, then suddenly drops. Their blood pressure plunges, and often they faint. Sarah* remembered that while she was in grade school, she would close her eyes during bloody movie scenes. That was not unusual, because other kids did the same thing. However, when she was about sixteen, she saw a newspaper photo of bloody palm prints. She fainted. Sometime later, during a history class movie, she fainted during a bloody scene.

Sarah then started fainting once a week. The fainting started to happen twice a week, then every day, until she was fainting every few hours. Sarah remembered, "The Gulf War was going on at that time, so magazines and newspapers were full of bloody images and ideas. In English class, we'd read stories in which people were injured, and those scared me. In biology class, talking about body parts made me faint. I think my imagination was too vivid!" She once even fainted when a teacher gave her back a test corrected with red ink!

Sarah's medical tests found nothing unusual. She got help from the Center for Stress and Anxiety Disorders at the State University of New York at Albany. The therapists tried various treatments with Sarah. First, she had to list situations, from the least frightening to the most frightening. Then she learned how to tense up, to keep her blood pressure from dropping, and to keep from fainting during a phobic reaction. Most people with phobias need to learn how to relax when they are afraid, but Sarah had to learn how to do the opposite. She practiced tensing her muscles while standing, sitting, and walking. Finally, the therapists had Sarah choose a piece of cheerful music.

Sarah's work on her phobia began. The first thing on her list was to write the word *blood* many, many times. She practiced her muscle tensing and listened to her

*Not her real name.

favorite music. Soon she was comfortable with writing *blood.* She then learned to look at raw meat, bloody pictures, and movies without feeling faint. After only three months, she no longer fainted or felt anxious at the sight or thought of blood.

"My final tasks were to have my blood drawn and to watch a hip operation. When I went to get my blood drawn, the doctor couldn't find my vein, so he let me draw his blood!" she said. She liked watching the hip operation. "I think the therapist who came along with me was more upset than I was." Now Sarah says she still feels a bit uncomfortable about blood and injuries, but she can handle herself just fine.[10]

Lachanophobia—"Eat your vegetables," mothers often tell their children. Some people, though, are afraid of vegetables. Some lachanophobics say that they cannot eat anything that has grown in the ground. Others fear that they are eating contaminated vegetables, because plants absorb pollutants from the water and air.

Microphobia—Germs, a general word for tiny organisms that cause disease, refers to bacteria and viruses. In addition to bacteria and viruses, people with microphobia can also fear molds and yeasts. Microphobics tend to keep themselves and their possessions ultraclean. They may also fear diseases.

Musicophobia, melophobia—Throughout history, certain types of music have been feared and, as a result, banned. For example, Adolf Hitler outlawed any music by Jewish composers during his reign in Germany. For decades, rock and roll music has been feared and disliked by some people. In the early 1950s, some cities banned rock and roll dances and concerts in public places, dance halls, and at swimming pools. Schools forbade it at dances and shows. During the 1960s, songs by the Beatles and the Rolling Stones were banned by some people because of the lyrics. Rock songs of the 1970s about sex, antiwar protests, and drugs were censored. Censorship of some popular music continues today by disc jockeys, record store owners, politicians, school officials, churches and other special-interest groups, and parents.[11]

People with a music phobia generally fear only one type of music, for example, organ music. Erica violently disliked rock music, although she once had liked it a lot. Her fear grew out of a horrible accident. One winter night, she was in a car with four other college students. The road was icy, and the driver lost control of the car and crashed through an embankment, killing four people trapped inside. Only Erica remained alive. She was stuck inside the car for hours, in terrible pain, with her four dead friends. The only sound she heard was the rock music coming from the car radio.

After she was rescued, Erica could no longer listen to rock music, although she had forgotten about the radio playing in the wrecked car. Soon, her dislike of rock music had grown to a phobia, and then it spread to any situations involving rock music such as parties, dances, and concerts.[12]

Musophobia, murophobia—Fear of mice or rats is a well-known and common phobia. Musophobics say their fear comes from knowing that rodents eat and destroy food. They associate mice and rats with dirt and disease and intensely dislike their small, black droppings. Rat bites can lead to rat-bite fever. This serious disease causes fever, chills, bad headaches, and rashes. Because

Most of us enjoy music, like these two girls at an old player piano. Yet some people fear music, usually a specific instrument, such as an organ or a piano.

these animals are tiny, they can hide in small places. Musophobics are terrified of mice or rats suddenly scurrying out at them. People who fear mice and rats try to avoid them. If they see one, they scream, jump, or run away from them, or even faint. Most musophobics develop their fear as young children.

Nosemaphobia, nosophobia—Some people with nosemaphobia or nosophobia worry about catching or having a specific illness or disease. This is different from hypochondria. Hypochondriacs are convinced that they are ill or are about to become ill. They worry about minor things like an occassional cough or sneeze. Fear of specific diseases changes over time, depending on what diseases are most common and terrifying. Today, nosemaphobics often fear death from: AIDS (Acquired Immune Deficiency Syndrome), cancer, heart disease, and venereal disease. As a result, they avoid anything that may remind them of the disease, including newspaper articles and television and radio programs. They often search their bodies for any signs of the disease and go to doctors for frequent tests. Fear of illness is most common among middle-aged and older persons and occurs in more women than men.

Numerophobia—Fear of numbers can take several forms. Some people fear certain numbers such as one or thirteen. (The fear of the number thirteen is called triskaidekaphobia.) Mathematics or working with numbers strikes fear into the hearts of some people. Taking a math test makes some people anxious. Others experience terror if they have to try to figure out a bus timetable or count change. Some people dislike getting numbers assigned to them. Social security numbers, work identification numbers, credit card numbers, even library card numbers can upset a numerophobic.

Nyctophobia—Young children sometimes fear the night. That is because they fear the unknown, the dark, or being separated from their parents and being alone. Children with nyctophobia imagine monsters under their beds, in their closets, or at their bedroom windows. Sometimes people are afraid that they will not wake up the next morning.

People who do not sleep well sometimes fear the night, especially if they have a hard time falling asleep, wake up during the night, or have nightmares. Nightmares often cause the person to wake up screaming. Luckily, most children outgrow their night terrors.

Occupational phobias—People sometimes develop phobias because of their work in dangerous jobs. Jim's phobia appeared immediately after his job accident. Jim, a miner, was at work four thousand feet below the surface of the earth. A large air current caused his safety helmet to fly into the bottom of an elevator shaft. Jim leaned in to get his helmet. Suddenly, the eight-ton steel elevator cage crashed down and pinned his head against the guardrails. After quite a while, the other miners freed him, and Jim was rushed to the hospital for surgery. He recovered physically, but he continued to have horrible nightmares about being in dark, closed-in places. After six weeks of treatment for his claustrophobia, Jim overcame it. [13]

Treatment has helped others overcome their occupational phobias, including a construction worker who fell five stories and became afraid of heights (acrophobia, hysophobia), and another man who was badly burned at work and could not stand to be near fire, not even a match (pyrophobia).

Ochlophobia, demophobia, enochlophobia—The fear of crowds, which includes fear of being with a large number of people in one place, is probably related to claustrophobia. If they are in a crowd, ochlophobics may fear that they cannot get out fast enough, or that there is no place that is safe with so many people around. Many people with agoraphobia also fear crowds.

Odynesphobia, odynophobia—No one likes or wants to be in pain, but some people develop extreme fears of even mild pain. An odynephobic will avoid seeing a doctor or dentist, or going to a hospital. Usually, odynesphobics worry more about avoiding physical pain than actually experiencing it.

Ombrophobia—Gardeners usually hope for rain so that their plants will grow well. People who fear rain will avoid even walking in it. They will check the weather regularly, and they try to avoid being outside when rain is predicted.

Ophidiophobia—One of the most common phobias of people throughout the world is of snakes. People cite several reasons for their fear: Snakes can bite them and cause illness; poisonous snakes can give them a fatal snakebite; snakes slither and look slimy; pythons and boa constrictors can crush people to death. Many people cannot tell a poisonous snake from one that is not poisonous. Poisonous snakes, while rare, do live in some parts of the United States.

Ornithophobia—People with this phobia often fear that a bird's sudden movements mean that the bird will attack them. Others say that the swooping movements and the sight and sound of flapping wings frighten them. The bird's small, beady eyes and sharp claws scare others. Many ornithophobics fear pigeons, since these birds live around buildings and people more than other birds do. Sometimes people only fear dead birds. Keith Schooler, referred to in Chapter 2, remembers when his ornithophobia began. "When I was about four years old, I was in the chicken coop, collecting eggs. Suddenly, all the chickens began running toward me. I felt trapped and scared. I just turned and ran out of there."[14] People with severe ornithophobia fear leaving their houses, walking outside, or traveling by car or bus. They keep all windows tightly closed. In extreme cases, people will not look outside, to avoid seeing any birds.

Papyrophobia—A fear of paper can include the fear of touching or seeing paper, being cut by paper edges, or thinking about paper. Any type of paper qualifies: wrapping paper, wallpaper, or drawing paper. Jack had a rare newspaper phobia. His fear was greater if the newspaper was damp. If he saw some torn, wet newspapers, he would have a phobic attack. A former politician, Jack kept his fear of newspapers a secret because he worried that his political opponents would ridicule him.

Jack wanted to run for Congress, but his fear of newspapers created a major problem: He needed to know the news, but he could not go near a newspaper. The news on television was not as precise as he needed his information to be. He had his employees summarize reports on what was happening in the news. He covered his fear by explaining that he "didn't have time to wade through the papers every day."

Although it is rare, some people are afraid of papers, which may include newspapers.

Jack said, "Ever since I can remember, I've been afraid to touch or be touched by a newspaper, or even to handle a newspaper clipping. And the sight of a wet paper, or the idea of coming into contact with wet newsprint, makes me nauseous. Sometimes people tap me with a paper and I just about faint." He had no fear of books, magazines, or other types of paper.

He avoided subways, because he was afraid of being brushed by someone carrying a newspaper. If he saw a newspaper stand or bundles of newspapers, he would race to the other side of the street. Jack has worked on his fear, though. He can now read a newspaper, but he can touch it with only one or two fingers.[15]

Public speaking—Phobias involving public speaking are the most widespread phobias in the United States. Also called stage fright or performance anxiety, this fear is actually a form of social phobia. Many people get sweaty hands or butterflies in the stomach in certain situations, particularly before and during public speeches and musical, dramatic, or other performances. This surge of fear, particularly before a performance, is common.

Over time, many people learn how to deal with their fears. Taking deep breaths before going on stage helps, as does positive thinking. Experience with performing or speaking in front of audiences tends to reduce anxieties.

Someone with severe performance anxiety has a persistent, irrational fear of being watched and judged by the audience. This phobia has affected the careers of talented musicians, actors, and other performers. Sometimes they may need help to deal with their phobia. Treatment with antianxiety drugs has been helpful for people such as musicians, public speakers, pilots, and athletes.

Scolinophobia—School phobics cannot go to school. This phobia usually starts during the grade school years and is equally common in girls and boys. Therapists often find that it is actually an exaggerated fear of leaving the home or parents. Many children display a wide range of symptoms that include headaches, vomiting, diarrhea, stomach pain, feeling faint, and a sore throat. Some may cry a lot. Children with school phobias are often embarrassed about their phobia and tend to avoid their friends.

Technophobia—A 1993 survey by Dell Computer Corporation found that more than half of all American adults fear technology. Twenty-five percent are unable to program their VCR or set their car radio buttons. The same percentage of people miss the manual typewriter. Over one third are uncomfortable using a car phone. Other pieces of technology that make people anxious are compact disc players, digital alarm clocks, programmable thermostats for furnaces, automatic teller machines, and computers. (Cyberphobia is a form of technophobia.) This study and another one by the New York Telephone Company showed that 45 percent of those surveyed did not want video or picture phones.

Technophobics may break into a sweat when they try to follow instructions to use a computer or VCR. Their blood pressure skyrockets. Others fear that machines will replace people. Studies show that younger people have less technophobia than do older people. "Technology is a sign of our times," said Dan Gookin, author of the computer book *Windows for Dummies.* However, he believes, "Technology has simply passed many people by."[16]

Triskaidekaphobia—Have you been in any tall buildings without a floor numbered thirteen? Because fear of the number thirteen is so common, some building owners skip this number. Triskaidekaphobics fear anything involving it, including apartment or house numbers, phone numbers, or the thirteenth day of the month. "My kindergarten teacher feared the number thirteen," Clay Bartl remembered. "My birthday is December 13, but she had the class celebrate my birthday on December 12. I was only six years old, and didn't understand her phobia. I had to ask my parents why she pretended my birthday was on the twelfth."[17]

Tropophobia, neophobia—People who fear moving or making changes generally like routines because they provide security. For some of these people, any changes in their jobs or changes in their routes to and from school or work can cause panic. New jobs or homes are particularly scary to these people. Moving to a new school involves a lot of changes, such as making new friends, getting to know the teachers, finding new clubs or activities, and so on. In extreme cases, tropophobics will not travel because they fear new places.

Vermiphobia, scoleciphobia—People who fear worms avoid going to places where worms are easily seen, such as bait stores, rivers, lakes, or swamps. Some people with this phobia will not go out on rainy days for fear of seeing worms.

Xenophobia—Babies and young children sometimes are afraid of strangers and react by crying or screaming. Researchers find that xenophobia is common from ages six to twelve months. Most of us outgrow this fear, but some people continue to avoid strangers. They also often fear parties and crowds (ochlophobia).

Zoophobia—Researchers find that many people fear animals. Zoophobics fear animals in general, while others fear wild animals (agrizoophobia) or particular animals such as snakes (ophidiophobia) or mice (musophobia). These phobias often develop while a child is young, from age four to eight. An attack by a rat, a dog bite, a scary movie about sharks such as *Jaws*, or hearing someone scream in reaction to a snake may start a young child on the path toward an animal phobia. Sometimes adults develop animal phobias as well.

People with zoophobia probably have never seen the live wild animals at a zoo. Animal phobias often develop around the age of four, but most people outgrow their animal fears.

69

5

What Causes Phobias?

No one knows what causes phobias, but researchers have developed many theories. To develop their theories, researchers first observe and listen to their patients, or they may measure patients' reactions in laboratory tests. They then develop theories and test them, either with phobic patients or in scientific experiments. So far, their experiments have shown that the causes of phobias are complex and often not well defined. The many theories are grouped into five categories: psychological, learned or conditioned, biological/chemical, cultural, and mixture.

Psychological Theories

Some researchers say that phobias arise when people ignore unresolved problems and conflicts. If someone has a stressful home life, for example, and never gets any help, then that person's anxiety will grow. Over time, that anxiety can change into a phobia. The phobia is the way that person manages the fearful situation. It symbolizes the real fear and allows the person to focus all fears onto one situation or thing.

Here is how this type of phobia developed for one person. A medical student always felt anxious when he took the subway to his classes. One day, he got angry at a professor during a class and stormed out. The next day, he stopped at the wide, busy street near the school but could not walk across it because he felt afraid. He got home by taking a subway and a taxi, so he did not have to walk across any streets. After that, this young man could not leave his home: He had developed agoraphobia. When he sought help, his therapist discovered that this man had never wanted to become a doctor; that had been his parents' dream for him. Family therapy resulted in three things: The young man left medical school, he returned to college, and he earned a degree in sociology, his real interest.[1]

One woman who could not leave her home realized during therapy that her agoraphobia had started after she was charged with shoplifting. For other people, agoraphobia often follows a severe shock, such as the death of a husband, wife, or close friend, or after a major event, such as surgery.

Social phobias often develop from complex causes. Many social phobics describe their parents as overprotective and highly concerned about others' opinions. Studies show that, when they were children, about 42 percent of agoraphobics had problems separating from their parents.[2] They became extremely anxious if their

71

A fear of death is one of the most universal fears. It may form the basis of many other phobias.

parents left home to go to work, or if they themselves had to go to school. Perhaps these people continued to carry their childhood separation fears with them, avoiding situations that separated them from loved ones.

This theory may explain why a death or major surgery may trigger agoraphobia. It also explains why some agoraphobics can leave their homes if a trusted person (a husband, wife, child, or close friend) goes out with them.

At age forty, Mrs. M. first began having panic attacks, which then developed into agoraphobia. She quit her job and would not leave her home for years. She focused her energies on worrying about her healthy, hardworking husband. Perhaps her agoraphobia started when Mrs. M. was a young child. Dr. Julian M. Herskowitz, director of Territorial Apprehensiveness (TERRAP), stated, "Overprotective parents can project their own fears onto the child and give them the feeling that the world is a dangerous place where anything bad can happen at any time. And when a spouse becomes overly concerned about the other partner, that is often an indication that the worry is really about oneself, about being left alone."[3] TERRAP is a phobia treatment center in Menlo Park, California.

Biological or Chemical Theories

Other researchers say that certain people develop phobias because of their body chemistry. These people are more likely to be fearful, to have panic attacks, and to develop phobias. Some researchers have found low levels of the chemical dopamine in the brains of phobics. In experiments with mice, those with low levels of dopamine react without much aggression. This theory seems to explain why some social phobics and agoraphobics have panic attacks.

Researchers can cause panic attacks by injecting certain chemicals, such as sodium lactate, into some people. After one panic attack, they are more likely to have them again if they are injected with the same chemicals. Some agoraphobics appear to have unusual brain chemistry and react differently to stress than do nonphobics. These people are also sensitive to some chemicals, such as caffeine. This drug is in coffee, tea, chocolate, hot cocoa, and many soft drinks.

Dr. Harold Levinson offers another theory. In his book *Phobia Free*, he writes that 90 percent of all phobias are caused by physical problems with the inner ear. He reports that medication for inner ear disorders, used with therapy, has helped many of his patients.

Other researchers say that phobics may have inherited a genetic predisposition to phobias. This means genes that can transmit certain characteristics were passed on from the parents to their children. No one knows what causes the phobia to grow in some people, but not in others. Dr. Marilyn Gellis, founder of Phobics Anonymous in Palm Springs, California, believes that people develop phobias because they have a chemical or genetic predisposition.[4] Arthur Henley, in his book, *Phobias: The Crippling Fears*, writes, "Theoretically, all of us may harbor a phobia 'germ' but in most of us it will remain dormant because something in our nature keeps it quiescent [quiet]."[5]

Genetic researchers have studied families to find out if heredity can determine who will develop phobias. Their studies show that certain phobias often run in families, especially agoraphobia and some specific phobias. A Norwegian study found that identical twins were more likely to have social phobias in common than were nonidentical twins. One researcher has found that people with relatives who have phobias are two to three times more likely to develop phobias themselves.[6] However, researchers cannot tell if this tendency is inherited or if it is learned by growing up around or living with a phobic. Although paralyzing fears can run in families, family members also can help each other overcome fears.

Some social phobics remember that they were easily scared when they were children, at age four or five. They hid from relatives who came to their homes, or they could not speak in class. Another trait many social phobics share is great sensitivity to rejection.

Learning Theories

Some researchers say that people learn fear through direct experience. Specific phobias sometimes develop from a scary situation or real danger. A person who is thrown from a horse may develop an intense fear of horses. If a child sees someone bitten by a snake or is continually warned to be careful of snakes, then the child may learn to fear snakes.

In the 1920s, J. B. Watson (1878–1958), an American psychologist, trained a young boy to fear rats (musophobia). Whenever a white rat was placed by the child, a loud noise blared. After a while, the boy

75

People may learn fear from direct experience. A fear of shadows (sciophobia) may be related to a fear of light or twilight (photophobia).

screamed when any rat appeared. His phobia grew to dogs, rabbits, and even a piece of cotton. Some researchers claim that Watson's cruel experiment shows that incorrect learning or conditioning can often result in a phobia.

Larry L. King, coauthor of a musical, remembers how his cynophobia (fear of dogs) grew. Until he was nearly three, Larry and his beloved dog, Shep, happily played together. Then Shep got rabies. Two men came to Larry's house and shot and killed his dog. The terrible memories of his pet's death remained in his mind, and Larry started to fear all dogs. At age eight, after he was viciously attacked by two large neighborhood dogs, he began to have nightmares about dogs. He arranged elaborate routes to get home from school so he could avoid any dogs. His dog phobia continued until he was married, with two children. Larry's mother-in-law asked him to look after Bandit, her small dog. Embarrassed to admit his phobia, Larry agreed. During a long afternoon, gentle Bandit managed to remind Larry that dogs can be fun and can provide good company. Larry's phobia finally dissolved when he and his family brought home their own dog, Buster.[7]

Cultural Theories

Another group of researchers point to culture as the cause of phobias. They think that the way people live, as well as the people, customs, and beliefs they grow up learning about, cause certain people to develop phobias. Cultures that allow people to express their fears and worries freely develop fewer phobics than do cultures

77

that insist that people hide their feelings. Some research has shown that there appear to be few phobias in Mediterranean cultures (Italian, Spanish, Arabic, and Greek). These cultures encourage people to display and discuss their feelings.[8]

Therapists point out, though, that not everyone who is attacked by a dog develops a dog phobia. Other people who never are hurt by a bird may develop a bird phobia after seeing a scary movie about birds.

Dr. Richard Macgraw points out, "Phobias are very common in childhood and are nearly universal."[9] Some researchers find that certain fears have always been known to people of all ages, throughout the centuries, across cultures. These universal phobias include the fear of snakes, mice, insects, and knives. These fears are a type of basic reaction to the sounds, colors, scents, shapes, or movements of these objects. Diane has an insect phobia. She explained, "I won't walk anywhere near trees. The sight of a caterpillar is enough to give me a heart attack—even a photograph of a caterpillar makes me panicky."[10]

Probably a Mixture

Researchers have performed many experiments to find the cause of phobias. No single theory has proven to be correct. Many researchers tend to think that simple phobias come from early experience and learning. Agoraphobia, and sometimes social phobias, seem to stem from biological causes. Most likely, all phobias develop from a mixture of causes.

6

Dealing With Phobias:
Treatment

Although we do not yet fully understand the causes of many phobias, treatments for phobias are usually very effective. The Anxiety Disorders Association of America reports that at least 90 percent of people with anxiety disorders, including phobias, report recovery or significant progress after treatment.[1] However, the National Institutes of Mental Health (NIMH) finds that only 23 percent of people with phobias actually get help or treatment.[2]

NIMH spends millions of dollars on research investigating the causes and treatments of anxiety disorders, including phobias. The type of treatment varies for each person and can include sessions with therapists, medication, self-help, and combinations of therapies. Treatment periods vary from a few months to a year or more. Most treatments focus on helping people cope with their phobic reactions so that they can control their fears and lead a fuller, happier life.

For most phobics, their fears follow a cycle. Usually they dread a feared situation or object, go to great lengths to avoid it, then try to ignore the tension produced from their fear and avoidance. Phobics need to learn to break their fear cycle. Some people can do this by themselves or with the help of a support group. Other people may need different types of treatment.

Mason's Story

Mason kept his fear of driving a secret from other people for many years. His real fear was that of humiliation. He worried that he could not parallel park, or would drive too slowly and make someone angry, or panic and lose control of his car and kill someone. "I couldn't stand being exposed as a failure. My heart would pound, I would get very nervous, and I would start to lock up whenever I even thought about driving," he said.[3]

"Most people think I must have had a bad experience driving when I was younger, but the truth is I was thirty-two years old before I ever got behind a wheel!" Mason finally got tired of making excuses and trying to find someone to drive him places. He decided that he needed to learn to drive. "I couldn't face the humiliation of asking one of my friends to teach me, so I signed up with one of those big driving schools. I figured if I couldn't stand the driving lessons, I would just quit. You know, just fade away quietly."[4]

At first, Mason tried to postpone his lessons, and he made all kinds of excuses to his instructor. The instructor kept pestering Mason to try. Mason said, "Finally, I had to give in and make an appointment or let my instructor know I was a real coward." Mason did go on to get his license. "Now I can actually talk openly about my fear of driving, acknowledge it, but not give in to it."[5]

Many people with phobias work around their fears and never deal directly with them. At some point in their life, some, like Mason, decide to fight their fears by themselves. Others may need some professional help. We know a lot about how to reduce stress and anxiety and how to build self-esteem. This knowledge can help people with phobias. Therapists and treatment programs also offer people individual or group treatments.

What Individuals Can Do By Themselves

Today people can go to any large bookstore or public library to find self-help books and workbooks on dealing with phobias and panic attacks. Some people work through the books by themselves. Others use them with a therapist.

Some people can help themselves by lowering their overall tension level. Their endless fear cycle increases their everyday tension and damages their self-esteem. By lowering their tension, some people lessen the chance that they will panic or have a phobic reaction. It also helps them better handle panic attacks if they occur. Here are some ways people can calm themselves before or during a phobic reaction:

Relaxation or meditation. Studies show that relaxation and meditation cause chemical changes in the brain that produce a feeling of peace and acceptance. These feelings

Phobics can turn to their public libraries to find a variety of self-help
materials on phobias, relaxation, and exercise.

are calming to someone with a phobia. Regular, deep breathing is a key aid, as is relaxing the muscles to lessen tension. People perform deep breathing and relaxing exercises before or during a phobic reaction. There are many self-help books and workbooks, television shows, videocassettes, audiocassettes, and classes that teach relaxation or meditation. Therapists often teach these techniques, too.

Positive imagery. People use reassuring, positive images and memories to relax themselves, which helps ward off phobic reactions. There are many self-help books, videocassettes, and audiocassettes that teach people about positive imagery. The technique is easy to learn.

Physical exercise. People who are constantly anxious build nervous tension. The body can discharge this energy through regular exercise, and this helps people deal with phobias. Physical exercise builds confidence, self-esteem, and a healthy feeling. Probably the easiest exercise that uses the large muscles of the body is walking. Swimming, jogging, bicycling, skating, tennis—any regular exercise will also give the mind and body a boost.

Learn acceptance. Experts say that phobics should not fight their feelings and fears. Acceptance helps people gain control over their phobias. Instead of negative self-talk such as "I look foolish" or "Everyone sees me sweating," people learn to substitute positive or accepting self-messages. Before phobic feelings develop, people can say things to themselves such as:

I look good today.
My class report is interesting.

If they feel a phobic reaction building, they can say positive, reassuring things such as:

I'm going to think slowly about this.

I don't like feeling this way, but I can accept it.

I can feel like this and still be OK.

This has happened before and I was OK. I'll be OK this time, too.[6]

Don't use drugs. Therapists recommend that people with a history of anxiety, including phobias, reduce their caffeine. Dr. Edmund Bourne advises that most people prone to anxiety or panic should keep their "total caffeine consumption to less than 100 mg [milligram]/day. For example, one cup of percolated coffee or two diet cola beverages a day would be a maximum. For those people who are very sensitive to caffeine, less than 50 mg/day would be advisable."[7] But perhaps eliminating caffeine altogether would be a good step to take.

Another way to reduce anxiety is to stop using alcohol, and tobacco. Some people try to manage their fears by drinking. However, using alcohol in this way may increase phobic episodes and may lead to alcoholism. Nicotine, the drug found in tobacco, can cause anxiety. Illegal drugs, including marijuana, cocaine, amphetamines, and PCP, can produce excessive anxiety and other phobic symptoms.

Skills Training

Schools teach academic subjects such as science, math, and history. But they generally do not offer classes on how to deal with everyday life. People need to know how to succeed at work and at school, handle stress, make and keep friends, succeed in marriage, raise children, and so on. Some people do not learn or develop these social skills. For others, living in a family where someone abuses alcohol or other drugs is stressful and often keeps family members from growing emotionally.

Various places offer low-cost skill training classes or seminars, including continuing education programs at colleges and universities, community colleges, junior colleges, community mental health centers, community education centers, health maintenance organizations (HMOs), churches, hospitals, and many training institutions. Classes and seminars number in the hundreds, and they include assertiveness training, self-esteem building, stress management, relaxation training, and grief and loss programs. Community education centers often offer teen programs. These classes and seminars are advertised in local newspapers, class catalogs, clinic waiting rooms, community and church bulletins, and special mailings.

National Agencies or Organizations

Scattered throughout the United States are organizations that offer education about phobias and also provide referrals to mental health treatment professionals, self-help groups, and other local resources.

Anxiety Disorders of America (ADAA)—Founded in 1980, this national organization in Rockville, Maryland, aids people with phobias and their families through education and information. ADAA publishes a variety of materials for people with phobias and also for health professionals who are treating those with phobias. ADAA does not recommend any one treatment and encourages people to check around and find what works best for the individual. This organization maintains an information clearinghouse on phobias and other anxiety disorders and provides a list of mental health professionals. The ADAA also operates a self-help network for locating local support groups.

National Mental Health Association (NMHA) —This group was founded in Alexandria, Virginia, by Clifford W. Beers in 1909. NMHA provides information on phobias and lists of mental health organizations that provide resources and information about self-help groups, treatment professionals, and community clinics. NMHA also works with the federal government to promote research and services for those people with mental health problems.

The National Institutes of Mental Health —The Panic Disorder Hotline is part of the federal Panic Disorder Education Program. The hot line staff will send callers lists of mental health treatment professionals and information about self-help groups and other resources. They publish information about panic attacks and phobias.

Support or Self-help Groups

Various support and self-help groups have sprung up throughout the United States. These organizations offer alternatives to therapy or are a supplement to therapy. These groups usually consist of people with phobias or other anxiety disorders and sometimes their families. The groups help members learn and share experiences. Groups that help people with phobias follow.

Phobics Anonymous—Dr. Marilyn Gellis founded The Institute for Phobic Awareness, Phobics Anonymous World Service Headquarters, in 1981. Located in Palm Springs, California, Phobics Anonymous, a branch of the institute, grew out of Dr. Gellis's own agoraphobia and recovery. She based Phobics Anonymous on the successful twelve-step program of Alcoholics Anonymous (AA). Her nonprofit, international organization, with more than one hundred twenty self-help groups, is open to anyone suffering from anxiety, panic attacks, phobias, and other anxiety disorders.

"We have no quick fix or cure. Just a process for improving the quality of life enabling the phobic to cope and become functional; thriving, not just surviving 'one day at a time,'" explains Dr. Gellis.[8] Small self-help groups meet once a week and are free. Sessions last about two hours and are run by a group member. Members are encouraged to call each other during the week.

Agoraphobics in Motion (AIM)—Since 1983, AIM has offered support to people with agoraphobia and related anxiety problems. This self-help program is available in eleven states. People can sign up for small group discussions and support, field trips, and relaxation technique courses.

Agoraphobics Building Independent Lives (ABIL)—is a network of support groups for people with agoraphobia and other phobias and panic-related disorders. Formed in 1986, ABIL has grown to twenty-eight self-help groups. ABIL offers members group meetings, a newsletter, and telephone links with other people with similar disorders. It is not affiliated with any religious organization, nor is it a therapy group. Instead, ABIL offers

87

members a place to set goals to overcome problems, share successes, and learn how to deal with setbacks.

Recovery, Inc.—Started in Chicago in 1937 by Dr. Abraham A. Low, Recovery has grown to include a thousand support groups throughout the United States. Recovery groups also meet in Canada, Puerto Rico, Great Britain, and Ireland. Recovery teaches people to deal with their phobic reactions through weekly support group meetings. This program helps people deal with crises, fears, panic, and anxiety. It emphasizes taking responsibility for oneself and learning self-confidence.

Recovery offers no medical advice and advises people to follow their doctors' instructions. No professionals are involved, and Recovery is not affiliated with any organizations or religion. One group leader explained, "We have limitations—no diagnosing, no counseling, and no giving advice at the meeting."[9] Held in a public place such as a library, church, or YMCA, each meeting opens with a reading or a taped lecture. Members then tell about using the Recovery method during the week. They also describe how they would have reacted before learning Recovery's methods. A question and comment period follows, and then members break into small groups for discussion.

Therapy

Therapists tailor treatment for each person. No one treatment works for all phobias, and people may want to try different ones. Jerilyn Ross, president of the ADAA, explains, "We're not at the point where we know which treatment works best for which people. It's a bit of trial and error."[10]

The length of treatment depends on the person, the phobia, and the treatment. Some people overcome their phobias in a few weeks, while others take months or longer. To determine if a treatment is helping, the ADAA advises that people should see some improvement within twelve to sixteen weeks. Most people do not go into a hospital for treatment; they visit a therapist's office for treatment sessions. The cost for treatment varies a lot. The ADAA estimates that a typical course of treatment runs about $2,000.[11]

When treating people with phobias, therapists generally use a combination of behavior therapy, cognitive therapy, and relaxation therapy. Behavior therapy helps people with phobias change and gain control over their unwanted behaviors. This therapy emphasizes that people change their behaviors based on knowledge they learn about themselves. Behavior therapists often teach people to cope by guiding them through exposure to feared situations or objects. Because people work on their own recovery, they develop skills that they can use after therapy ends. In cognitive therapy, which was developed in the 1960s, people first analyze their feelings. They learn to separate realistic and unrealistic thoughts, then change their thought patterns. The goal is to change self-defeating or distorted thoughts.

Relaxation Therapy includes various techniques. Deep breathing probably ranks as the most important. People learn to breathe slowly and deeply from the diaphragm. This helps during peiods of "fight or flight" because breathing tends to become shallow and rapid, which adds to panic. People also find progressive relaxation of the body's muscle groups relaxing. Thinking of calming thoughts or repeating a simple word or phrase may also help ward off a panic attack. Yoga is also a form of relaxation therapy.

Many therapists combine behavior and cognitive therapy, along with relaxation training, when treating phobias. The goal in behavior therapy is for the person actually to confront the feared situation or object and to learn that nothing horrible happens. To do this, the person goes through a series of graded steps, often beginning with an imagined step, then continuing through successive steps to the real situation itself. Cognitive therapy, used with behavior therapy, teaches people to quiet the thoughts that feed the phobia. These therapies are used once a week for ten to twenty-four sessions.

Here is an example of how combined therapy works. Art Decker, a licensed psychologist in St. Louis Park, Minnesota, has provided therapy for many people since 1980.

> Self-talk in dealing with phobias is important. Instead of panicking, I teach each person that 'I have options.' I help people find the base of their fears, then look at reality and what is rational and what is irrational. Ultimately, I have them face their fears, and do whatever they're afraid of doing.
>
> For example, a person came to me for help because of his social phobia. A social phobia is an intense fear of not knowing what to say or do with strangers. This person was beyond shy. He was afraid of being with people and couldn't push himself into social situations.

I had him draw up a list from one to ten of what he considered a little fearful all the way up to frightening. He would try to carry out each step over ten weeks. Meantime, I helped him build on his success by starting small, with nothing overwhelming. The first week he said "Hi" to a co-worker. Over time, he took a class, then attended an anxiety-phobia group. I taught him how to relax before and after each of these key events. He also learned deep breathing and muscle relaxation. Finally, he achieved his goal—he went to a party.[12]

Medication

Medications must be prescribed by a doctor and they generally are used only for people with severe phobias. The ADAA stresses that medication must be used along with other forms of therapy. Art Decker points out, "Medications can help some people, but they are not a cure-all. Even if you use medications, ninety percent of the time you still have the phobia."[13]

In the early 1960s, researchers discovered that some antidepressants could prevent the panic attacks of agoraphobics. Although scientists are not certain how these drugs work, the idea is that once panic attacks are gone, the agoraphobic will be less anxious and start to recover.

Today, doctors prescribe three types of antidepressant drugs for people with severe phobias: tricyclic antidepressants, monoamine oxidase inhibitors (MAOIs), and selective serotin reuptake inhibitors (SSRIs). These drugs are usually used to help people with depression, but they also decrease anxiety. Some people find that a low dose works. For others, a higher dose is needed, equal to that needed to reduce depression. Most people find that they can stop taking their medications within six to twelve months. Doctors sometimes prescribe an antidepressant to help performers with severe stage fright. The performers take their medication as needed.

Antidepressants can cause unwanted side effects, such as drowsiness, jittery feelings, or a dry mouth. People taking MAOIs must watch their diets, avoiding aged cheese, many types of alcoholic beverages, smoked meats and sausages, and so on. Reactions between these foods and the MAOIs can produce very high blood pressure, severe headaches, other side effects, and may lead to strokes. SSRIs include fluoxetine, sertraline, paroxetine, venlafaxine, fluvoxamine, and nefazadone. Researchers find that some people who have panic attacks have low serotonin levels. The brain's nerve cells use seratonin as a chemical messenger to transmit information back and forth. If serotonin levels are low, nerve cells misfire or slow down. SSRIs keep the right amount of serotonin in the brain by preventing the body from reabsorbing it. SSRIs affect only serotonin; they do not change other brain chemicals. The most widely known SSRI is Prozac™, which is the name brand of the drug fluoxetine.

National Treatment Programs

Several programs are nationally recognized for their variety of treatments. In a typical program, people with phobias work together in groups with a trained group leader. The groups meet once a week, and sometimes family members and friends attend. During the group sessions, people learn new attitudes and skills to help them overcome their phobias.

Each person also has a weekly practice session, either alone or in a group, with a therapist. During these sessions, the person uses the new coping skills in situations that were formerly avoided. Sometimes the therapist stays with the person during these situations. When setbacks occur, more practice is needed. Some agoraphobics who are housebound begin their treatment in their own homes.

Although these national programs have helped people with phobias across the United States, not everyone can easily get to them, so some national programs also offer home study courses. Others, like PASS-Group, conduct telephone counseling. To find therapists or treatment programs in your area, you can call or write the American Psychological Association, the American Psychiatric Association, the American Association for Counseling and Development, the National Mental Health Association, or the ADAA. The "Where to Go for Help" section in the back of this book may also be helpful.

Territorial Apprehensiveness (TERRAP) was founded in 1962 by Dr. Arthur B. Hardy. Located in Menlo Park, California, it focuses on the causes and treatment of anxieties, fears, and phobias, especially agoraphobia. TERRAP provides information and counseling for those with phobias through group education and treatment. People with phobias meet weekly for up to sixteen weeks. Professionals run the meetings. TERRAP also offers a home study course and private instruction. For people unable to leave their homes, a TERRAP therapist will come to the home.

Freedom From Fear (FFF) was established in Staten Island, New York, in 1984. This program aids and counsels people with phobias, fears, depression, and anxieties. In 1986, FFF became affiliated with the Department of Psychiatry of the College of Physicians & Surgeons of Columbia University. Together, they run a large research and treatment center in Staten Island.

Midwest Center for Stress and Anxiety, Inc., was founded by Lucinda Bassett after she overcame her social phobia, as well as her fears of driving and flying. She has developed a fifteen-week home study program that has been used by many people worldwide. The Midwest Center is located in Oak Harbor, Ohio.

PASS-Group, Inc. offers a twelve-week program given by telephone—not necessarily because clients are home-bound (90 percent are not), but because this was found to be an effective, low-cost way of providing individualized help. Counselors must be recovered panic attack sufferers, because the founder believes that they make the best "teachers." They encourage their clients to take the same approach that made them well: A seven-step program that includes good nutrition, exercise, and a change of attitude. There are PASS-Group counselors in various cities; the home office is in Williamsville, New York.

The Phobia Clinic at White Plains Hospital Center in New York offers various treatments for people with phobias. People can attend Phobia Self-Help Groups. These groups meet regularly for ninety minutes each week and are run by trained phobia aides. Another therapy choice is the 8 Week Phobia Clinic. This consists of eight weekly ninety-minute group meetings with a psychiatrist and group leader and a one-hour-per-week session with a phobia aide. For those who can travel to and stay in the White Plains-area for one to two weeks, the Phobia Clinic offers an Intensive Course. All treatments focus on helping people deal with their fears through contextual therapy, the study and treatment of the phobia in the setting in which the phobic reactions occur. The Phobia Clinic was started in 1971 by Dr. Manuel Zane.

Morton Silverman, a phobia aide at The Phobia Clinic at White Plains Hospital Center, describes how he helped one man overcome his fear of vacations: Silverman was assigned to work with a famous professor who taught at a graduate school. While on vacation, the professor awoke from a nap aboard a yacht and had the first phobic reaction of his life. "When he opened his eyes he saw, only two inches from his nose, the bottom of the bunk above his. He felt smothered, trapped and he panicked. Heart pounding, sweating, and trembling, he raced out on deck, breathing hard and struggling for breath."[14]

The professor returned to work, and months passed without any more incidents. Then, while he was on vacation at Disney World in Florida, the professor had another phobic reaction while he was in a plastic bubble ride. He became terrified and climbed right over people to get out of the bubble. Although his phobia did not interfere with his work, he started to worry about traveling on a boat, or airplane, or in a crowded car. He came to the Phobia Clinic for treatment.

Silverman had a problem carrying out the treatment for the professor. "We could not find a place to practice in which he had fear levels," he explained.[15] The professor needed to learn how to control his fear in the same or similar situations. Then Silverman remembered that the professor described his phobia as feeling as if he were in a coffin. He asked the professor if being in the trunk of a closed car would cause him to feel the phobic reactions. The professor said "yes," and treatment started.

During treatment, the professor learned new skills that he could use to handle his fears. Meanwhile, during each treatment session, he allowed Silverman to close the trunk lid a little more, until it was shut. By this time, the professor did not hesitate to get into the car trunk and have Silverman shut him in. After eight weeks, the treatment had worked. The professor has enjoyed phobia-free vacations for many years.[16]

Dealing Successfully with Phobias
There is a lot of help available today for people with phobias and most people can be successfully treated. They can use many self-help techniques or seek various types of professional help. Check the "Where to Go for Help" section for more information.

Where to Go for Help

Many organizations offer information, treatment, and support relating to phobias and other anxiety disorders.

INFORMATION

American Psychiatric Assocation
1400 K Street, NW
Washington, DC 20005
(202) 682-6000

American Self-Help Clearinghouse
St. Clare's-Riverside Medical Center
Denville, NJ 07834
(201) 625-9565

Anxiety Disorders Association of America (ADAA)
6000 Executive Boulevard
Rockville, MD 20852-3801
(301) 231-9350

Council on Anxiety Disorders
P.O. Box 17011
Winston-Salem, NC 27116
(919) 722-7760

Life Skills Education
314 Washington Street
Northfield, MN 55057
(800) 783-6743

National Institutes of Mental Health (NIMH)
Information Resources and Inquiries Branch/
Publications List
Room 15C-05
5600 Fishers Lane
Rockville, MD 20857
(301) 443-4513

National Mental Health Association (NMHA)
1201 Prince Street
Alexandria, VA 22314-2971
(703) 838-7500

The National Panic/Anxiety Disorder Newsletter (NPAD News)
1718 Burgundy Place
Suite B
Santa Rosa, CA 95403
(707) 527-5738

TREATMENT

Agoraphobics Building Independent Lives (ABIL, Inc.)
1418 Lorraine Avenue
Richmond, VA 23227
(804) 266-9409

Agoraphobics in Motion (A.I.M.)
1729 Crooks
Royal Oak, MI 48067
(313) 547-0400

Freedom From Fear (FFF)
308 Seaview Avenue
Staten Island, NY 10305
(718) 351-1717

Midwest Center for Stress and Anxiety, Inc.
P.O. Box 205
106 North Church Street
Suite 200
Oak Harbor, OH 43449
(800) 944-9440

PASS-Group
6 Mahogany Drive
Williamsville, NY 14221
(716) 689-4399

Phobia Clinic at White Plains Hospital Center
Davis Avenue at East Post Road
White Plains, NY 10601-4699
(914) 681-0600

Phobics Anonymous World Service Headquarters
P.O. Box 1180
Palm Springs, CA 92263
(619) 322-COPE

Recovery, Inc.
Headquarters
802 North Dearborn Street
Chicago, IL 60610
(312) 337-5661

TERRAP Programs
932 Evelyn Street
Menlo Park, CA 94025
(415) 327-1312

Chapter Notes

Chapter 1

1. "A Teenager's Struggle with Panic Disorder," *Quest: A Newsletter of the Council on Anxiety Disorders,* Summer 1994, p. 2; Linda Robbian, "The Effect of Panic Disorder on Two High School Students," *Quest: A Newsletter of the Council on Anxiety Disorders,* Fall 1994, pp. 1–2.

2. Joe Eltgroth, personal interview, St. Paul, Minn., August 23, 1994.

3. Harry Milt, "Phobias: The Ailments and the Treatments," [booklet], (New York: Public Affairs Committee, Inc., 1987), pp. 2–3.

4. American Psychiatric Association, "Facts About: Phobias," [booklet] (Washington, D.C.: American Psychiatric Association, 1992), p. 1.

5. Susan Chollar, "Fear Itself," *Woman's Day,* May 18, 1993, p. 68.

6. Life Skills Education, "You & Your Phobias," [booklet], (Northfield, Minn.: Life Skills Education, 1992), p. 4.

7. Elizabeth Stark, "Quicker Fixer Uppers," *American Health,* October 1991, p. 44.

8. Chollar, p. 68.

9. Jerilyn Ross, *Triumph over Fear* (New York: Bantam Books, 1994), p. xvii.

Chapter 2

1. Susan Chollar, "Fear Itself," *Woman's Day*, May 18, 1993, p. 70.

2. Amanda Warren, "Scare Tactics: Living with Your Secret Fears," *Mademoiselle*, October 1991, p. 98.

3. Cathy Perlmutter, "5 Who Conquered Fear," *Prevention*, July 1992, p. 105.

4. Ibid., p. 57.

5. American Psychiatric Association, "Facts About: Phobias," [booklet], (Washington, D.C.: American Psychiatric Association, 1992), p. 1.

6. Joan W. Anderson, "High Anxiety," *Ladies Home Journal*, February 1992, p. 100.

7. Keith Schooler, personal interview, St. Paul, Minn., August 23, 1994.

8. C.B. Serighar, *From Panic to Peace of Mind: Overcoming Panic and Agoraphobia* (New Orleans: Bruno Press, 1991), p. 95.

9. Stephen Garber, Marianne Garber, and Robyn Spizman, *Monsters Under the Bed and Other Childhood Fears* (New York: Villard Books, 1993), p. 175.

10. Jerilyn Ross, *Triumph over Fear* (New York: Bantam Books, 1994), pp. 36–37.

11. Ibid., p. 34.

12. American Psychiatric Association, p. 1.

13. Jack Maser, "Anxiety Disorders—America's Most Common Mental Health Problem," *ON TARGET: Newsletter of Freedom From Fear, Inc.*, Spring 1994, p. 1.; Lesley Jane Seymour, "Fear of Almost Everything," *Mademoiselle*, September 1993, p. 252.

14. Maser, p. 1.

15. Ibid.

16. Carol Schatz, "Drive Me Crazy," *Mademoiselle,* October 1991, p. 100.

17. The Institute for Phobic Awareness, *From Anxiety Addict to Serenity Seeker: Interpreting and Working the 12 Steps of Phobics Anonymous* (Palm Springs, Calif.: The Institute for Phobic Awareness, 1993), p. 42.

18. Anxiety Disorders Association of America, *Phobias,* [booklet], (Rockville, Md.: Anxiety Disorders Association of America, 1991), p. 5.

19. The Institute for Phobic Awareness, pp. 164, 165.

20. Mark S. Gold, *The Good News About Panic, Anxiety, and Phobias* (New York: Bantam Books, 1989), p. 37.

21. Carol Schatz, "Fear of Almost Everything," *Mademoiselle,* September 1993, p. 252.

22. Gold, p. 39.

23. Arthur Henly, *Phobias: The Crippling Fears* (New York: Avon Books, 1987), p. 12.

24. Ibid., pp. 11–12.

25. Gold, p. 39.

26. "Cat People," *Catnip,* Tufts University School of Veterinary Medicine Newsletter, July 1994, p.8.

27. Gold, p. 39

28. Ronald M. Doctor and Ada P. Kahn, *The Encyclopedia of Phobias, Fears, and Anxieties* (New York: Facts on File, 1989), p. 198.

29. Fraser Kent, *Nothing to Fear: Coping with Phobias,* (Garden City, N.Y.: Doubleday, 1977), pp. 6–7.

Chapter 3

1. Fraser Kent, *Nothing to Fear: Coping with Phobias* (Garden City, N.Y.: Doubleday, 1977), p. 11.

2. Ronald M. Doctor and Ada P. Kahn, *The Encyclopedia of Phobias, Fears, and Anxieties* (New York: Facts on File, 1989), p. 312.

3. Ibid., p. 313.

4. Ibid.

5. Lesley Jane Seymour, "Fear of Almost Everything," *Mademoiselle*, September 1993, pp. 252–253.

Chapter 4

1. Fraser Kent, *Nothing to Fear: Coping with Phobias* (Garden City, NY: Doubleday, 1977), pp. 71–72.

2. Hillary Michael Quinn, "Fright Flight," *Mademoiselle*, October 1991, p. 101.

3. Ronald M. Doctor and Ada P. Kahn, *The Encyclopedia of Phobias, Fears, and Anxieties* (New York: Facts on File, 1989), p. 12.

4. Kent, pp. 36–37

5. Carol Murray, personal interview, Little Canada, Minn., October 10, 1994.

6. Tony Whitehead, *Fears and Phobias: What They Are and How to Overcome Them* (New York: Arco, 1983), p. 23.

7. Ibid., pp. 22–23.

8. Bonnie Leir, personal interview, St. Paul, Minn., August 12, 1994.

9. Doctor and Kahn, p. 128.

10. Cathy Perlmutter, "5 Who Conquered Fear," *Prevention*, July 1992, pp. 107–109.

11. Judy Monroe, *Censorship* (New York: Macmillan, 1990), pp. 16–18.

12. Harry Mitt, *Phobias: The Ailments and the Treatments* [booklet], (New York: Public Affairs Committee, 1908), pp. 18–19.

13. Kent, pp. 75–76.

14. Keith Schooler, personal interview, St. Paul, Minn., October 19, 1994.

15. Kent, pp. 77–78.

16. Robert S. Boyd, "Technophobia May Prove Pothole on the Information Superhighway," *St. Paul Pioneer Press,* May 8, 1994, pp. 1A, 11A.

17. Clay Bartl, personal interview, South St. Paul, Minn., October 29, 1994.

Chapter 5

1. Tony Whitehead, *Fears and Phobias: What They Are and How to Overcome Them* (New York: Arco, 1983), pp. 34–35.

2. Alcohol, Drug Abuse, and Mental Health Administration, "Useful Information on Phobias and Panic," [booklet], (Rockville, Md.: U.S. Department of Health and Human Services, DHHS Publication No. [ADM] 88–1472, 1988), p. 16.

3. Arthur Henley, *Phobias: The Crippling Fears* (New York: Avon Books, 1987), pp. 28–29.

4. Marilyn Gellis, personal interview, Palm Springs, Calif., May 28, 1994.

5. Henley, p. 49.

6. Lesley Jane Seymour, "Fear of Almost Everything," *Mademoiselle,* September 1993, p. 254.

7. Larry L. King, "Thanks, Buster" *Parade Magazine,* May 8, 1994, pp. 18–19.

8. Life Skills Education, "You & Your Phobias," [booklet] (Northfield, Minn.: Life Skills Education, 1992), p. 9.

9. Midwest Health Institute, *Phobias,* [audiocassette], (Minneapolis, Minn.: Midwest Health Institute, 1990).

10. Harold L. Levinson and Steven Carter, *Phobia Free* (New York: M. Evans and Company, 1986), p. 168.

Chapter 6

1. Anxiety Disorders Association of America, *Consumers' Guide to Treatment,* [booklet], (Rockville, Md.: Anxiety Disorders Association of America, 1991), p. 1.

2. Jerilyn Ross, *Triumph over Fear* (New York: Bantam Books, 1994), p. 23.

3. Mark S. Gold, *The Good News About Panic, Anxiety, and Phobias* (New York: Bantam Books, 1989), p. 246.

4. Ibid., pp. 246–247.

5. Ibid., p. 247.

6. Life Skills Education, "You & Your Phobias," [booklet], (Northfield, Minn.: Life Skills Education, 1992), pp. 11–12.

7. Edmund J. Bourne, "Caffeine," *ON TARGET: Newsletter of Freedom from Fear, Inc.,* May 4, 1994, p. 7.

8. Marilyn Gellis, "Phobics Anonymous," [booklet], (Palm Springs, Calif.: The Institute for Phobic Awareness, 1991).

9. Donald J. Dalessio and Robert L. Goldstein, "Group Helps You Fight Fear, Depression," *San Diego Tribune,* February 20, 1990.

10. Lesley Jane Seymour, "Fear of Almost Everything," *Mademoiselle*, September 1993, p. 254.

11. Anxiety Disorders Association of America, p. 3

12. Art Decker, personal interview, St. Louis Park, Minn., April 26, 1994.

13. Ibid.

14. Morton S. Silverman, "It Sounded Exciting to Me," *P.M. News: Special 20th Anniversary Issue* (White Plains, N.Y.: Phobia Clinic of White Plains Hospital Center, September/October 1991), p. 7.

15. Ibid.

16. Ibid.

Glossary

agoraphobia—The avoidance of a particular place or situation because of the fear of having a panic attack there.

alcoholic—Someone who is addicted to alcohol.

alcoholism—A disease in which a person has an overwhelming desire to drink alcoholic beverages.

antianxiety medications—Drugs that prevent or relieve uneasy feelings.

antidepressant medications—Drugs that prevent or relieve persistent feelings of sadness or despair. They are often used for panic attacks.

anxiety—A feeling of unease and distress that may not be related to any particular object or situation.

behavior therapy—This treatment helps people change and gain control over their unwanted behaviors.

cognitive therapy—This treatment helps people change their self-defeating or distorted thoughts.

contextual therapy—The study and treatment of a phobia in the actual setting in which the phobic reactions occur.

fear—A feeling, usually short-lived, of alarm or fright caused by real or imagined danger or pain.

genetics—A branch of biology dealing with heredity.

hypochondriac—Someone who is convinced that he or she is ill or is about to become ill and often feels real pain when there is no physical illness present or likely.

MAOIs—Monoamine oxidase inhibitors, drugs that helps people decrease their anxiety.

panic—A sudden, overwhelming terror.

panic attack—A sudden, unexplained period when a person reacts to an extreme fear, although there is no cause for fear.

phobia—An irrational, intense fear of an object or situation.

phobic—A person who has a phobia.

Phobos—A Greek war god who spread terror and fear among his enemies.

prescription—A doctor's orders or instructions for taking a drug.

psychiatrist—A physician specializing in disorders of the mind.

psychiatry—The medical study, diagnosis, treatment, and prevention of mental illness.

relaxation—Making the body or mind less rigid, tight, or tense.

shyness—A bashful feeling; a discomfort around strangers.

simple phobia—An unreasonable, persistent fear of an object or situation. The most common simple phobia is fear of animals.

social phobia—An intense fear of situations in which the person could be watched and judged by others.

superstition—The belief that an object, action, or circumstance will influence the outcome of an unrelated event.

therapist—Someone trained to provide treatment for illnesses, disabilities, or other conditions.

therapy—Treatment to help someone overcome an illness, disability, or other condition such as a phobia.

tricyclic antidepressant—A drug that helps people decrease their anxiety.

universal phobia—An irrational fear that many people have had throughout the centuries, especially of snakes, mice, and insects.

Further Reading

Doctor, Ronald M., and Ada P. Kahn. *The Encyclopedia of Phobias, Fears, and Anxieties* (New York: Facts on File, 1989).

Garber, Stephen, Marianne Garber, and Robyn Spizman. *Monsters Under the Bed and Other Childhood Fears* (New York: Villard Books, 1993).

Gellis, Marilyn, and Rosemary Muat. *The Twelve Steps of Phobics Anonymous* (Palm Springs, CA: The Institute for Phobic Awareness, 1989).

Gold, Mark S. *The Good News About Panic, Anxiety, and Phobias* (New York: Bantam Books, 1989).

Greist, J. H., and J. W. Jefferson. *Panic Disorder and Agoraphobia: A Guide* (Madison: Anxiety Disorders Center and Information Centers, University of Wisconsin, 1992).

Institute for Phobic Awareness, The. *From Anxiety Addict to Serenity Seeker: Interpreting and Working the 12 Steps of Phobics Anonymous* (Palm Springs, CA: The Institute for Phobic Awareness, 1993).

Levinson, Harold L., and Steven Carter. *Phobia Free* (New York: M. Evans and Company, 1986).

Ross, Jerilyn. *Triumph over Fear* (New York: Bantam Books, 1994).

Index